Most Things Spurgeon
A DAILY DEVOTIONAL

COMPILED AND FULLY UPDATED
FOR TODAY'S READERS

BY

ROGER MCREYNOLDS

Abbreviations

NASB — *The New American Standard Bible*
NKJV — *The New King James Version*
TNSDB — *The New Spurgeon's Devotional Bible*

ALSO UPDATED BY THE EDITOR

Charles Haddon Spurgeon

According to Promise: The Lord's Method of Dealing with His Chosen People

All of Grace (including larger 16-point font paperback)

Peace and Purpose in Trial and Suffering

Spurgeon's Catechism: Updated for Today's Reader and Using the ESV

The Clue of the Maze: 70 Daily Readings for Conquering Doubt + 3 Sermons

The Imprecatory Psalms from The Treasury of David (February 2019)

The New Spurgeon's Devotional Bible: A 600,000 Word Two Year Devotional

The Soul Winner (August 2019)

Spurgeon's Sermons Series

3:16: Thirteen Selected Sermons

A Defense of Calvinism: Including 7 Sermons on the Doctrines of Grace

A Sower Went Out to Sow: Nine Sermons on The Parable of the Sower

Lost and Found: 10 Evangelistic Sermons

Other Works

Sermons of D. L. Moody: 21 Sermons

The Fear of God, by John Bunyan

The Reformed Pastor, by Richard Baxter (April 2019)

Contact Information

MostThingsSpurgeon@gmail.com

www.goo.gl/kLbXcU

Editor's Introduction

Over the past several years, we have been updating works of Charles Spurgeon for today's readers. Along the way we have also updated *The Fear of God* by John Bunyan as well as a book of sermons by D. L. Moody. Last year, we began taking brief quotes from these updated works and posting them on a Facebook account called *Most Things Spurgeon.* Several readers suggested we compile them in book form. This book is the result.

Included in these updated works are some of the Psalms from Spurgeon's *The Treasury of David.* Virtually all of the quotes not from Spurgeon, Bunyan, and Moody are taken from this work from the section of each Psalm titled *Explanatory Notes and Other Comments* where Spurgeon cites numerous other writers.

The brief quotes we have included between some days are all from Spurgeon, unless otherwise indicated.

The aim of this book is to help enrich and grow the saints. "For I did not shrink from declaring to you the whole counsel of God" (Acts 20:27). Christians should be thinking people. We have not confined our quotes to tender, uplifting ones—as important as they are. The practical side of faith in Christ also deals with the heart that "is deceitful above all things, and desperately sick" (Jeremiah 17:9). The godly men quoted here were doctors of the heart. Many were pastors; they knew their own hearts and the hearts of others. They used the living and active word of God that discerns the thoughts and intentions of the heart in their ministries to their people (Hebrews 4:12). Like them, we would not be faithful to you unless we were faithful about "declaring to you the whole counsel of God" (Acts 20:27).

WHAT IS YOUR RELATION WITH CHRIST?

Everything depends on your answer to this question. Are you depending on Christ alone? Then the Lord has promised to bless you, and do you good; and he will surprise you with the amazing ways in which he will do this for you. Nothing is too good for the Father to give to the person who delights in his Son Jesus.

On the other hand, are you trusting in your own works, feelings, prayers, and rituals? Then you are under the works of the law, and you are under the curse. Do you remember what we said about the offspring of Hagar, the slave woman? Guess what your portion will be if you remain in slavery to sin? Oh, that you would leave the house of slavery, and flee to the home of free grace, and become one whom God will bless. —*According to Promise*

You have promised this good thing to your servant.

—2 Samuel 7:28b

King David knew what the Lord had promised to give him, and he referred to it in his prayer as "this good thing." We need to be more serious in our praying by being more specific than we usually are. We pray for everything in such a general way that we practically pray for nothing. It is good to know what we want. This is the reason our Lord said to the blind man, "What do you want me to do for you?" He wanted him to be aware of his own needs, and to be filled with eager desires regarding those needs. These are valuable ingredients in composing our prayer.

—*According to Promise*

They say that Christians should be one, and they should; but I go further, and assert that all who are in Christ are already one. When our Lord prayed, "That they may all be one" (John 17:21), was he not heard? Was his prayer ineffective? I believe it was answered, and that to this day there is a vital family tie among all the people of God in every place. And though they sometimes try to hide that family unity, yet the love of Christ will win out and bring them together. Put two mere theologians together and they will fight like cats; but bring two spiritual men together at the cross and they will lie down like two lambs. They cannot help it; they must love each other in Christ. There is, there must be, an essential unity among those who are born again by the Holy Spirit. I rejoice and glory that the name, the person, and the work of Jesus are at the center of true Christianity.

—Sermon #1621 *The Ark of the Covenant*

Prayer has mercy running close behind it.

JANUARY 4

We have our hope set on the living God, who is the Savior of all people, especially of those who believe. —1 Timothy 4:10b

All mankind gains some benefit from Jesus' death. They are spared, they enjoy the common blessings of providence, and they enjoy the fact that the Lord controls everything in the universe. But redemption has its own special advantages that are reserved only for believers. The Savior's death and resurrection has purchased some good things for all people and all good things for some people. Are we believers? If we are, then Jesus is our Savior in a special sense. —*TNSDB*

Great…is the mystery of godliness. —1 Timothy 3:16

Even those who do not believe the facts of our religion cannot argue about the unspeakable greatness of them if they are true. Whatever status a person may have reached, if they are reasonable, they will admit that Christianly does not deal in trifles. Like the eagle, that does not hunt for flies, Christians set their sights on conquering the highest themes of thought. Right or wrong, the subjects with which we deal are not secondary. They are clothed with awe inspiring interest that only the foolish despise. Among teachers, Jesus is second to no one.

— Sermon #786 *The Great Mystery of Godliness*

RISE HIGHER

A man had just come from the East, and he had heard one of his friends talk about a beautiful sunrise, and he made arrangements with the proprietor to take him up on the summit to see the sunrise. So in the morning the guide woke him and they started out. The guide went ahead and he followed. He said they had not been gone a great while when there came a terrible thunder storm, and the old man said to the guide, "It will be no use to go up; we can't see the sun rise; the storm is fearful." "Oh, sir," said the guide, "I think we will get above the storm." They could see the lightning playing around them, and the great old mountain shook with the thunder, and it was very dark; but when they got up above the clouds all was light and clear.

So if it is dark here, rise higher; it is light enough up around the throne. —D. L. Moody, *God is Love*

WHAT HAS DOUBT ACHIEVED?

Why has no trophy ever been given to honor unbelief? Will we ever see the poet who praises doubt or the historian going on about skepticism? If so, what will they say? The "peaceful fruit of righteousness" and "obtained promises" are not in keeping with doubt. Enduring great amounts of suffering "so that they might rise again to a better life" is not something doubt inspires. Unbelief sneers at the mention of such a hope. The person who would praise doubt will have to be content with lesser achievements than the heroes found in The Book of Hebrews. What accomplishments can unbelief honor? What hospitals or orphanages has doubt built? What missions to cannibal tribes has infidelity maintained? What fallen women or ruined men has skepticism rescued and changed?

> Sing, muse! If such a theme, so dark, so wrong,
> May find a muse to grace it with a song.
>
> *—The Clue of the Maze*

But God, being rich in mercy, because of the great love with which he loved us, even when we were dead in our trespasses, made us alive together with Christ—by grace you have been saved and raised us up with him and seated us with him in the heavenly places in Christ Jesus. —Ephesians 2:4-6

That little sentence, "By grace you have been saved," is the key of true theology. Study it well, and believe it thoroughly, and you will escape a thousand doctrinal errors. Carry this text in your heart and you will be correct in your understanding of the faith.

By nature, we care about the things of this world, but grace sets us up above all earthly things. What sort of people ought we to be who sit with Jesus in heaven! *—TNSDB*

A great multitude that no one could number. —Revelation 7:9

I believe there will be more in heaven than in hell. If anyone asks me why I think that, I answer, because Christ is to have superiority in everything. I cannot imagine how he can have the supremacy if there will be more in Satan's territory than in paradise. And, I have never read that there is "a great multitude that no one could number" in hell. I rejoice in knowing that the souls of all infants, the moment they die, speed their way to paradise. Think what a vast multitude of them there is! Then there are the countless millions of "the spirits of the righteous made perfect" already in heaven—the redeemed "from every nation, from all tribes, and peoples and languages" until now. And there are better times coming, when the religion of Christ will be universal; when—

> "He shall reign from pole to pole,
> With limitless sway;"

—A Defense of Calvinism

THE LOWER THE HEART DESCENDS, THE HIGHER THE PRAYER ASCENDS.

A spiritual prayer is a humble prayer. Prayer is asking for charity, and that requires humility. "The tax collector, standing far off, would not even lift up his eyes to heaven, but beat his breast, saying, 'God, be merciful to me, a sinner!'" (Luke 18:13). God's glory is beyond the reach of human intellect and may even amaze us and strike a holy fear into us when we approach close to him: "O my God, I am ashamed and blush to lift my face to you" (Ezra 9:6). It is proper to see a poor nothing overwhelmed and lying flat at the feet of its Maker. "Behold, I have undertaken to speak to the Lord, I who am but dust and ashes" (Genesis 18:27). The lower the heart descends, the higher the prayer ascends.

—Thomas Watson (1620-1686)

He will quiet you by his love.

—Zephaniah 3:17

You have seen a mother wash her child, and as she washes its face the child is crying, because it does not enjoy the momentary cleansing operation. Does the mother share the child's distress? Does she cry too? Oh, no. She rejoices over her child, and rests in her love, because she knows this slight momentary affliction of the little one will work for its real good. Our distresses are often no more than the cry of a child because of the soap in its eyes. While the church is being washed with tribulations and persecutions, God is resting in his love. You and I are becoming impatient, but God is quiet and resting.

—Sermon #1990 *A Sermon for the Present Time*

Filled with all the fullness of God.

—Ephesians 3:19b

What an incomparable expression! We have here not only an indwelling God, but God in the greatest fullness of his Godhead filling and overflowing the entire soul with his fullness. I cannot help borrowing an illustration from a friend who took up a bottle by the seashore, filled it full of seawater, corked it, and then threw it into the ocean. "Now," said he, "there it is. There is the sea in the bottle and there is the bottle in the sea." It is full to fullness, and then it is still in a greater fullness.

There is my soul with God in it, and there is my soul in God. The fullness of God in me as much as I can hold, and then myself in the fullness of God. The illustration gives one as much of the text as one knows how to communicate. We are swallowed up in the all-consuming ocean of God's love, and that same love of God is flowing into all the parts and powers of our soul until we are as full of God as a human being can be.

—Sermon #707 *Heavenly Geometry*

Pray Without Ceasing.

—1 Thessalonians 5:17

Satan has three titles mentioned in the Scriptures, describing his enmity against the church of God: a dragon, referring to his evil intentions, a serpent, to describe his cunning, and a lion, to explain his strength. But none of these can stand before prayer. The greatest vengefulness of Haman sinks under the prayer of Esther; the strongest counsel of Ahithophel, withers before the prayer of David; and an army of a thousand Ethiopians, run away like cowards before the prayer of Asa. —Edward Reynolds (1599-1676)

THE GREAT GOD RESPONDS TO FAITH

We may not refuse to rely on God and use the excuse that we are too insignificant. It is not plausible that anything can be too little for God. The wonders of the microscope are just as remarkable as those of the telescope. We may not set a limit to the Lord in one direction and not the other. He can and will show his divine skill in a person's life, as well as in a planet's orbit. Witnesses are alive to testify to the Lord's baring "his holy arm" for those who trust him. Anyone may put the principle to the test; none have done so in vain. There are no reasons in his nature why God should not respond to his creature's confidence in him. There are many reasons why he should. At any rate, as far as we are concerned, we are ready to put faith to the test, and to let the experiment last throughout our entire existence.

—*The Clue of the Maze*

Has he spoken, and will he not fulfill it?

—Numbers 23:19

Many Christians do not treat the promises of God as if they were real, and this is a serious weakness. If a friend makes them a promise, they believe it, and look for its fulfillment. But they often look on God's promises as so many words that mean very little. This is very dishonoring to the Lord, as well as being very harmful to us.

You can be sure that the Lord does not consider his words of little importance. "Has he spoken, and will he not fulfill it?" He keeps his commitments. God speaks intentionally; his words are powerful and have meaning. We may depend on his words, there is no reason to question them—they will be fulfilled as certainly as they were spoken. Has anyone who trusted the Lord been disappointed? Can a single instance be found where our God has not kept his word? The ages cannot produce a single proof that the promise making Jehovah has been unfaithful to his word.

—According to Promise

ABOUT GETTING DISCOURAGED WHEN YOU SIN

You know they say short accounts make long friends. Keep short accounts with God. You should see the face of God every morning before you see the face of any human being. If you come to the cross every morning, you will never get further than one day's travel from the cross. You must say to yourself, "I want to feed my soul a breakfast every morning as well as my body. I want to see the face of God before I see the face of any person on earth." Just keep close to the cross and close to Jesus, and if anything has gone wrong during the day or evening, do not sleep until that account has been settled. Take it to Christ and tell it right out to him; tell him how you are sorry, and ask him to forgive you. He delights to forgive. That is what I mean by keeping a short account with God. —D. L. Moody, *Message to Young Converts*

Beloved, we are God's children now, and what we will be has not yet appeared; but we know that when he appears we shall be like him, because we shall see him as he is. —1 John 3:2

The Lord takes pleasure in those who fear him, imperfect though they are. He sees them as they will be, and he rejoices over them, even when they cannot rejoice over themselves. When your face is marred with tears, your eyes are red with weeping, and your heart heavy with sorrow for sin, the great Father is rejoicing over you. The prodigal son wept in his father's bosom, but the father rejoiced over his son. While we are questioning, doubting, sorrowing, and trembling, God rejoices. He sees the end from the beginning and knows what will result from our present anxieties and he "rejoices over you with gladness."

—Spurgeon Sermon #1990 *A Sermon for the Present Time*

Hear a just cause, O LORD. —Psalm 17:1

The troubled heart craves for the ear of the great Judge; it is persuaded that when God hears, the matter is set right. If our God could not or would not hear us, our situation would be indeed miserable. Yet some who profess religion place such small value on coming to the throne of grace that God does not hear them for the simple reason that they neglect to pray. We might as well have no house if we continue to live in streets and fields; we might as well have no God if we are always defending our own cause and never going to God. There is more fear that we will not hear the Lord than that the Lord will not hear us. —*The Treasury of David*

I will betroth you to me forever. I will betroth you to me in righteousness and in justice, in steadfast love and in mercy. I will betroth you to me in faithfulness. And you shall know the LORD. —Hosea 2:19-20

A marvelous promise! A bottomless gold mine of love. It is more appropriate to enjoy it in silence than to try to find words to explain it. Blessed are those who are married to the Lord. His love does not change. His wedding vows will never end in divorce.

—TNSDB

It is meanness itself to flatter the wealthy.
True religion lifts us above such littleness.

FAITH AND THE END

The Lord Jesus has promised to return to earth, and faith clings to this promise. Sometimes faith hopes that Jesus will return soon so that death will be avoided; but times and seasons have little effect on faith, because all the blessings of the return of Christ will be hers one way or another. If the Lord should come quickly, so that we do not see death, "We shall all be changed," and if he delays, and we die, "The dead will be raised imperishable." In either case "We will always be with the Lord." Therefore whether we live or die makes no difference to the heart of the believer. He says, "If I live, Christ will be with me; if I die, I will be with be with Christ." How slight the difference! *—The Clue of the Maze*

BRIGHTNESS BEFORE DARKNESS
DARKNESS BEFORE BRIGHTNESS

I have noticed, in the typical events of Christian experience, that our greatest joys come just after some of our severest trials. When the howling storm has played out its strength, it soothes itself to sleep. Then comes a time of calm and quiet, so great in its stillness, that only the monstrous storm could have been the mother of such a mighty calm.

This seems to us to be almost normal. Deep waves of trial, then high mountains of joy. But the reverse is true almost as often. Like Moses, we go from the top of Pisgah to our graves. One moment we are the top of Mount Carmel, the next we are going down to the dens of lions or to fight the leopards. Let us be on our guard, and not be like Manoah who, having seen the angel of the Lord, thought that he would surely die (Judges 13:2-24).

—Sermon #440, Cheer for the Fainthearted

Let us have grace, by which we may serve God acceptably with reverence and godly fear. —Hebrews 12:28 NKJV

The Lord God is the Maker of us all and he will be either our Savior or Judge. This text should be given serious consideration. We should pay attention to the words; we should be careful to accept them and put them into practice because they place before us the mighty God and call us to the highest duty toward him. That is, they tell us to fear him. I call it the highest duty, because it is not only a duty in itself, but, it is also the salt that seasons every responsibility we have to God. There is nothing we can do that is accepted by God unless it is seasoned with godly fear.

—John Bunyan, *The Fear of God*

"Therefore I tell you, do not be anxious about your life, what you will eat or what you will drink, nor about your body, what you will put on. Is not life more than food, and the body more than clothing? Look at the birds of the air: they neither sow nor reap nor gather into barns, and yet your heavenly Father feeds them. Are you not of more value than they?"

— Matthew 6:25-26

Do not stress out and worry about these less important things. God who gives us our life and bodies will give us food and clothing. Martin Luther (1483-1546) was walking in the fields one day during a difficult time in his life. He had his Bible in his hands, and reading the Sermon on the Mount, he found much comfort when he read Matthew 6:26. Just then a little bird was hopping from branch to branch, with its sweet chirping music, seeming to say,

"Mortal, cease from toil and sorrow,
God provides for tomorrow."

It then came to the ground to pick up a crumb and rising merrily, again seemed to repeat its simple song—

"Mortal, cease from toil and sorrow,
God provides for tomorrow."

This gave the Reformer's heart great comfort. —*TNSDB*

THE CHRISTIAN IS A MISSIONARY

The person who has believed in Jesus will be hopeful for others. This hopefulness is a great help in doing good. Many have failed to save others because they do not believe that they can be saved. Genuine Christians will give up on no one, because they themselves have found grace. The Word of God, which had power over their own minds, can just as easily influence others. They would attempt to convert the Pope or the Grand Imam if they had the opportunity; but, lacking that possibility, they set to work on whoever present themselves. A living faith is a reproducing faith. If you have no concern for the soul of your neighbor, it is time that you had a fear about your own soul. —*The Clue of the Maze*

JANUARY 25

Forgetting what lies behind and straining forward to what lies ahead, I press on toward the goal for the prize of the upward call of God in Christ Jesus. —Philippians 3:13a-14

"FORWARD" is our marching order. We never think of ourselves as good enough. We are far from being satisfied with what we have accomplished by divine grace. Our ultimate goal is far greater than anything we have yet done. We are still beginners in our Lord's school of grace. We hope to do far better things. We must be committed to spiritual things. To be early to work and late to prayer is not healthy. How dare we be busy in our own job and lazy in God's vineyard; awake in the world of business and asleep in the life of the church. "So run that you may obtain it." He who wants holiness, happiness, and heaven, must be in the race for them. —*TNSDB*

JANUARY 26

My righteous one shall *live* by faith. —Hebrews 10:38

A life of faith is always very different; it often seems very foolish to unsaved people. People who act by faith often seem to be acting carelessly in the eyes of the world. They appear to be impractical, because they do not follow the established principles of the day, but stick with those rules that God has given us for all time. Faith and patience often encourage a person to go the very way that caution and common sense would say is wrong. Those who are weak in the faith will often hold up their hands in astonishment, even if they do not speak with some measure of irritation, at the daring way in which people strong in faith challenge the promise of God, and act as though it were already fulfilled. —Spurgeon Sermon #440 *Cheer for the Fainthearted*

By faith Noah, being warned by God concerning events as yet unseen, in reverent fear constructed an ark for the saving of his household. By this he condemned the world and became an heir of the righteousness that comes by faith. —Hebrews 11:7

It was God's Word that warned Noah about things to come. That Word formed the faith that produced the reverent fear in his heart that caused him to prepare for unseen dangers and he became an inheritor of unseen happiness. Where there is not faith in the Word of God, this fear cannot exist. Where the Word does not make this good impression, this faith cannot exist. Like evil hangs together as links of a chain, so the graces of the Spirit and the fruits they produce depend on each other. One cannot be without the other. No faith, no fear of God. Devil's faith, devil's fear. Saint's faith, saint's fear. —John Bunyan, *The Fear of God*

BE VERY STRONG

Therefore, be very strong...that you may not mix with these nations remaining among you or make mention of the names of their gods or swear by them or serve them or bow down to them, but you shall cling to the LORD your God just as you have done to this day." —Joshua 23:7-8

Joshua compliments them as well as commands them. A little well deserved praise makes people all the more ready to listen. Joshua's lesson was: Separation from Sinners. It is a lesson that has not gone out of date and needs to be repeated to the church today. —*TNSDB*

FAITH PRAYS

The believing man always turns to God so that he can keep up his fellowship with the divine mind. Prayer is not a monologue, but a dialogue. Prayer is not self-analysis, but a lifting up of the "eyes to the hills," from where our help comes. There is a relief in confiding in a sympathetic friend, and faith feels this abundantly; but prayer is more than this. When we have followed the will of God in a project, and have done everything we can, and yet the goal has not been achieved, then the hand of God is trusted to go beyond what we have done, just as it was relied on to go with us during the activity. Faith has no desire to have its own will when that will is not according to the mind of God. God's wisdom is our best guide, but inappropriate desires do not rely on that; the urging of unbelief is at the bottom of such cravings. Faith knows that God's will is for the highest good, and that anything needed to reach that highest good will be given in answer to our prayers. Everything is already ours through God's loving gift. Prayer is the check by which we draw on our own bank account with God. The believer has the awareness of limitless riches without the danger of them. —*The Clue of the Maze*

With God all things are possible. —Matthew 19:26

The all-powerful God never promises beyond his ability. We often intend to act according to our word, but we find ourselves mastered by overwhelming circumstances. We are unable to keep our word and our promise is left unfulfilled. It can never be that way with the Almighty God, because his ability is limitless.

—According to Promise

Lay up for yourselves treasures in heaven. —Matthew 6:20

People talk about a man who died worth so many millions. It doesn't make any difference how much a man accumulates. He can't die worth anything, because he leaves it here. He is not worth a penny; and so, if you want to save your money, lay it up in heaven where thieves cannot get hold of it. Instead, make yourselves rich by investing in good organizations.

I have gotten sick and tired of going to men and begging for money. I hope the Lord of heaven will stir up people so that they will be going around to see where they can invest their money. I want to be rich for eternity, not for time. But how blind and shortsighted are people who are seeking to be rich just for time. People accumulate millions just to make the way to hell easy for their children. —D.L. Moody, *Message to Christian Workers*

Greediness is its own plague and brings other evils with it.

What if God, desiring to show his wrath and to make known his power, has endured with much patience vessels of wrath prepared for destruction, in order to make known the riches of his glory for vessels of mercy, which he has prepared beforehand for glory? —Romans 9:22-23

That God predestines, and yet that man is responsible, are two facts that few can clearly see. They are believed to be inconsistent and contradictory, but they are not. The fault is in our weak discernment. Two truths cannot contradict each other. So, if I find, in one part of the Bible, that everything is foreordained, that is true; and if I find, in another Scripture, that man is responsible for all his actions, that is true. It is only my lack of understanding that leads me to imagine that these two truths can ever contradict each other. I do not believe that they can ever be joined here on earth, but they certainly will be one in eternity. —*A Defense of Calvinism*

Whatever does not proceed from faith is sin. —Romans 14:23

Some people ask me questions about their daily walk and behavior. They say, "I would like to know whether it is right for me to go the theater?" "I would like to know whether it is right for me to smoke?" or, "to drink in moderation?" I cannot be your conscience; Christ does not lay down rules; he lays down principles. One rule I have had is this: If there is anything that troubles my conscience, and I am uncertain whether it is right or not, I give Christ the benefit of the doubt. It is better to be a little too strict than too liberal. And let me say to you young converts and you Christians here, the eyes of the world are on you; they are watching.

—D.L. Moody, *Message to Young Converts*

FEBRUARY 3

Has he spoken, and will he not fulfill it? —Numbers 23:19

Let us *know* the promises. Should we not have them at our fingertips? Should we not know them better than anything else? The promises should be the classics of believers. If you have not read the latest book, and have not heard about the most recent law passed by Congress, yet you should know correctly what God the Lord has said, and be anticipating its fulfillment. We should be so well versed in Scripture that we always have the promise that most exactly meets our case on the tip of our tongue. We ought to be transcripts of Scripture; the divine promise should be written on the pages of our hearts as much as it is on the pages of the Book.

—According to Promise

FEBRUARY 4

Pray without ceasing. —1 Thessalonians 5:17

Brothers and sisters, would you wish to warm the egg of unbelief until it hatches into a serpent? Then refuse to pray! Would you see evils grow larger and mercies grow smaller? Then refuse to pray! Would you see tribulations increased sevenfold and your faith decreased to the same degree? Then refuse to pray! I declare to you today, if you neglect praying, then all the troubles you have ever had will be as nothing compared to what will yet come on you. The little finger of your future doubts will be thicker than the thighs of your current mental torment. You will discover what a person is capable of when they leave their God. You will find out in the bitterness of your soul what an evil thing it is when people have forsaken "the fountain of living waters, and hewed out cisterns for themselves, broken cisterns that can hold no water."

—Sermon #439 The Danger of Doubting

FEBRUARY 5

> "'Tis a point I long to know,
>> Oft it causes anxious thought,
>> Do I love the Lord or no,
>> Am I his, or am I not?"

I think there are few Christian who never doubted. I think you might travel a great distance before you would meet with any. May God keep me from speaking lightly about unbelief! It is the most damnable of sins. May God prevent me from saying a word in favor of doubting or encouraging anyone to praise it. There cannot be a greater wickedness out of hell than doubting the promise of God. There cannot be a greater act of treason than to not trust the love, the faithfulness, the tenderness, the truth of the God who has helped us to this point. Still, we must admit, humiliating though it is, we do know that even those believers, whose hearts are true, sometimes find their strength failing them. Yes, even those who are clad in the armor of heaven are sometimes not dressed for action. —Sermon #440 *Cheer for the Fainthearted*

FEBRUARY 6

O you of little faith, why did you doubt? —Matthew 14:31

The law of gravity is constant, and so is the law of divine faithfulness. There are no exceptions to the rule that God will keep his covenant. Extreme cases, difficult cases, even impossible cases, are included within the parameters of the Lord's word. Therefore no one need despair, or even doubt. God's opportunity comes when a person's limit is reached. The worse the case, the more certain it is to be helped by the Lord. Oh, that my hopeless, helpless reader would do the Lord the honor to believe him, and leave everything in his hands! *—According to Promise*

For each will have to bear his own load. —Galatians 6:5

Each of us has his own load of responsibility to deal with. Therefore we would do well to remember our own faults and sympathize with the faults of others. When we are tempted to condemn others, we should consider our own failings. —*TNSDB*

May the glory of the LORD endure forever;
may the LORD rejoice in his works. —*Psalm 104:31*
If the Lord rejoices in his works, we would not
be wise to close our eyes to nature's beauties
or think they just happened by some huge accident.

HEAVEN AND THE NEW JERUSALEM
ARE NOT PLACES FOR LIARS

Nothing unclean, and no one who practices abomination and lying, shall ever come into it. —Revelation 21:27 NKJV

Outside are the dogs and sorcerers and the sexually immoral and murderers and idolaters, and everyone who loves and practices falsehood. —Revelation 22:15

Liars do not fear God. A habit of lying and the fear of God cannot stand together. This sin of lying is a common sin and walks in the world in several shapes and forms. There is the foulmouthed liar who wants to hurt others, there is the scheming liar who exaggerates, there is the hypocritical religious liar, and other liars in between. None of them will escape the damnation of hell unless they repent; because "all liars, their portion will be in the lake that burns with fire and sulfur" (Revelation 21:8).

—John Bunyan *The Fear of God*

SCIENTIFIC THEORIES ARE NOT INFALLIBLE

Those who have addicted themselves to the study of Nature, and have despised the Bible, certainly cannot claim they have never been mistaken. To demand a revision of Scripture every time they enthrone a new theory is the height of hypocrisy. The history of philosophy and science reads like a Comedy of Errors. Each generation of scholars has been highly successful in refuting all of their predecessors; and there is every probability that much of what is now approved as scientific doctrine will be entirely out of favor in a few years' time. —*The Clue of the Maze*

Nothing brings God to his children's rescue
like the attacks of their enemies.
Fathers cannot bear to hear their dear ones abused.

FEBRUARY 10

Remember also your Creator in the days of your youth, before the evil days come and the years draw near of which you will say, "I have no pleasure in them" — Ecclesiastes 12:1

Youth is the best time for serious thinking about important things and deciding to believe on Jesus. Old age robs much of the incentive and ability to consider the crucial subject of eternity. The mind is not as sharp as it used to be and the body is weakening. Both make examining subjects that have been ignored for a long life all the more difficult to consider. Young people should beware of delay and give up the idea that they can wait until they are older to think about giving their lives to Jesus. No tree is so easily bent as the green sapling. —*TNSDB*

SALVATION BELONGS TO THE LORD —Psalm 3:8

If one dear saint of God can perish, then all might perish. If one of the covenant ones can be lost, then all may be lost. If that can happen, then there is no true gospel promise, the Bible is a lie, and there is nothing in it worth accepting. I would immediately become an infidel when I can believe that a saint of God can ultimately fall. If God has loved me once, then he will love me forever. God has a master plan. He arranged everything in his gigantic intellect long before he did it; and once having decided it, he never changes it. —*A Defense of Calvinism*

Let me assure you, in God's name, if your religion has
no better foundation than your own strength,
it will not stand at the day of judgment.

O LORD…, to you the helpless commits himself. —Psalm 5:14

Every morning leave yourself and your ways in God's hand, as the psalmist phrases it, commit yourself to him. And at night look again how well God has kept that trust, and do not sleep until you have reminded your heart of his faithfulness, and then committed the night also to his care…. And by doing so, and with God's blessing, you will keep your faith in good condition for a longer race, when called to run it. —William Gurnall (1617-1679)

FEBRUARY 13

For the LORD your God will bless you, as he promised.

—Deuteronomy 15:6

In my times of trouble, I like to find a promise in the Bible that exactly fits my need, and then to put my finger on it, and say, "Lord, this is your word. I am asking you to prove that it is by carrying it out in my case. I believe that this is your own writing; and I ask you to make it good according to my faith." I believe in the unconditional inspiration of the Bible, and I humbly look to the Lord for an unconditional fulfillment of every sentence that he has put on record. I delight to hold the Lord to the very words that he has used, and to expect him to do just as he said, because he has said it. —*According to Promise*

The Lord often uses the most unlikely ways to help his people.

FEBRUARY 14

Then the Lord God said, "It is not good that the man should be alone; I will make him a helper fit for him."

—Genesis 2:28

Before Adam knew that he wanted a companion, his tender Creator knew it and had already decided to provide him one. The Lord looks into the future and his grace supplies our needs in advance. —*TNSDB*

BRINGING HOLINESS TO COMPLETION

God's presence and his name are held in awe and fear by his church. This includes our worship of him and our service for him. While we live in this world we are encouraged to conduct our worship in dread and fear. This is what David had in mind when he said, "But I, through the abundance of your steadfast love, will enter your house. I will bow down toward your holy temple in the fear of you" (Psalm 5:7). David also said, "Serve the LORD with fear" (Psalm 2:11). To praise God is part of worshiping him, but Moses reminds us, "Who is like you, majestic in holiness, awesome in glorious deeds, doing wonders?" (Exodus 15:11). To rejoice before him is a part of worshiping him, but David warns us to "rejoice with trembling." All of our service for God, and every part of that service, should be done with reverence and godly fear. Therefore, "Let us," as Paul says, "cleanse ourselves from every defilement of body and spirit, bringing holiness to completion in the fear of God" (2 Corinthians 7:1).

—John Bunyan, *The Fear of God*

When I look at your heavens, the work of your fingers,
the moon and the stars, which you have set in place,
what is man that you are mindful of him,
and the son of man that you care for him?

—Psalm 8:3-4

The heavens are so infinite and man is so small. The moon is so bright and man is so dull. The stars are so glorious and man is so insignificant. Lord, how can you stoop from the magnificence of heaven to visit such a nothing as man? The study of astronomy humbles the mind as well as expands it. Examining the heavens should excite adoring gratitude when we see how generous the Lord's love is to such insignificant creatures as ourselve*s*.

Yet you have made him a little lower than the heavenly
beings
and crowned him with glory and honor. —Psalm 8:5

Since man is mortal and angels are immortal, man is a little lower than they are right now. But in the future that will change when man is crowned with glory and honor. Then it shall be seen that angels are actually servants to the saints and that all creatures work for their benefit. —*TNSDB*

FEBRUARY 17

O LORD, you hear the desire of the afflicted. —Psalm 10:17

Prayer is presenting our desires to God in the name of Christ, for things that agree with his will. It is asking for divine favor upon our *desires*. Desires are the heart and soul of prayer; words are simply the body. Now as the body without the soul is dead, so are prayers unless they are motivated by our desires. "O LORD, you hear the desire of the afflicted." God does not hear words, but *desires*. —Thomas Watson (1620-1686)

FEBRUARY 18

TRUST IN THE LORD

If we trust in good people, then we should trust in the good God infinitely more. Why does it seem odd to trust in the promise of God? To many, it looks like a dreamy, sentimental, religious business; but if we consider it calmly, it is the most matter of fact action that can be.

God is real; everything else is like a shadow. He is certain; everything else is questionable. God must keep his word. This is absolutely necessary, how else could he be God?

—According to Promise

"When the bow is in the clouds, I will see it, and remember the everlasting covenant between God and every living creature of all flesh that is on the earth." —Genesis 9:16

The sign of the promise is seen in cloudy times when faith needs a reminder of the Lord's faithfulness the most. If there is no cloud, there is no rainbow. It is worth having a cloud to have God paint a rainbow on it. God seeing the rainbow is better than man's seeing it, because God will never see it with forgetful eyes.

God made the rainbow to be a lovely symbol of his truthfulness. It is a bow unstrung, because war is over. It is a bow without a string, because it will never be used against us. It is a bow turned upward, so that we may direct our thoughts and prayers to heaven. It is a rainbow of bright colors, because joy and peace are revealed by it. Blessed arch of beauty, always be the Lord's preacher to us.

—TNSDB

Nothing can stop the plans of God. In his plans there is a dark place for the rebel as well as a bright spot for the believer.

By faith Abraham, when he was tested. —Hebrews 11:17

The faith of Abraham was tested in many fires and ours will be too. Will it stand the test? Are we resting on the faithfulness and the power of almighty God? Anything less strong than this will fall out from under us. The faith of God's elect, which is the gift of God and the work of the Holy Spirit, will hold up, conquer and land us safely in the promised inheritance. Do we have this faith or not? May the Lord give us this most precious grace. *—TNSDB*

**"With long life I will satisfy him
and show him my salvation."** —Psalm 91:16

God's righteous saints may live many years or few, but how long we live is not what matters. The good we achieve and the fellowship with God we enjoy are what are most important.

As a family, let us thank God for protecting us from serious illness, from sudden death, and from fatal accidents. God has promised to be involved in our lives. The privilege of coming to God in prayer and the promise of being accepted by him when we do are two of the most precious things he has given us. If we are really God's children, then a guard of angels is hovering over us right now. We may rest assured that whatever dangers are near us, we are kept safe under the wings of God. Therefore, as Christians, we should be very calm in difficult times, and show by our holy courage that we have a definite reason for our confidence.

—TNSDB

WHEN JOSEPH'S BROTHERS RETURNED FROM EGYPT
WITH GRAIN DURING THE FAMINE

Then their father Israel said to them..., "Carry back with you the money that was returned in the mouth of your sacks. Perhaps it was an oversight." —Genesis 43:12

Before they left Egypt, "Joseph gave orders to fill their sacks with grain, and to replace every man's money in his sacks." His brothers did not know how the money got there and were therefore under obligation to return it. This was the right and honest thing to do. We are not permitted to take advantage of the mistakes of others. Every honest man will do what he can to correct mistakes that cause someone a loss, even though the error was not his.

—TNSDB

HIGHER

I was told about a little child who lay dying. As its breath grew faint, she said, "Lift me, papa." And he put his hand under the child and lifted her a little; and then she whispered "higher," and he raised her higher, and she still said "higher," and again "higher, higher," until he lifted her just as high as his arms could reach, until at last her heavenly Father lifted her into his eternal kingdom.

So our prayer should be, "Higher, higher, nearer my God to Christ." Everyday we should make a day's march toward heaven, and nearer and nearer to him.

—D. L. Moody, *Message to Young Converts*

In due season we will reap, if we do not give up.

—Galatians 6:9

There are delays in the answers to our prayers. As the farmer does not harvest today what he sowed yesterday, so neither do we always immediately receive from the Lord what we are asking from him. The door of grace does open, but not to our first knocks. Why is this? It is because the mercy will be all the greater for being longer in coming. There is a time for every purpose under heaven, and everything is best in its time. Fruit ripens in its season; and the more seasonable it is the better it is. Premature mercies would be only half mercies; therefore the Lord withholds them until they have reached perfection. Even heaven itself will be the better because it will not be ours until it is prepared for us, and we are prepared for it. —*According to Promise*

My righteous one shall live by faith. —Hebrews 10:38

A person may glide into disbelief without realizing it, and remain comfortable once there; but to believe is to be alive, to be alert and prepared for conflict. Those who think faith is child's play will need to take great strides towards mature adulthood before they are capable of testing their own beliefs. Shall we prefer doubt over belief because it is so easy, or shall we become truth seekers even if it means we have to plunge into the depths like pearl divers? We will choose our rule of life according to the spirit within us. A brave soul will resist the dishonorable way of the crowd and pursue the higher paths even if they are more difficult. —*The Clue of the Maze*

[Jesus] told this parable: "A man had a fig tree planted in his vineyard, and he came seeking fruit on it and found none.

It was in good soil and under the gardener's care. Therefore it would produce fruit or prove to be good for nothing.

And he said to the vinedresser, 'Look, for three years now I have come seeking fruit on this fig tree, and I find none. Cut it down. Why should it use up the ground?'" —Luke 13:6-7

Three years was long enough for a test. There might have been two bad seasons to account for the absence of fruit, but when the tree was fruitless a third time the fault must be in the tree itself. God gives us enough time to be tested. God has allowed all of us enough time to prove ourselves. Perhaps this is the moment the Lord is saying, "Cut it down." Some of us are like this barren fig tree. By itself it is of no use. If fills the place where a good tree could be planted. It draws nutrients from the soil and hurts other trees that are near it. In the same way some people live useless lives, and at the same time they are in positions that others could be in who would bring glory to God. —*TNSDB*

The Lord God took the man and put him in the garden of Eden to work it and keep it. —Genesis 2:25

Some kind of work is necessary to be happy. Lazy people would not enjoy even the garden of Eden itself. A perfect man is a working man. —*TNSDB*

Let us not expect easy times. We are servants of a Master who was surrounded by disapproval and died on a cross. How can we expect those who crowned Him with thorns to crown us with roses?

O LORD, who shall sojourn in your tent?
    Who shall dwell on your holy hill?
He...who does not slander with his tongue
    and does no evil to his neighbor. —Psalm 15:1-2

The person who lives in the presence of God is too brave to say something behind a man's back that he would not say to his face. He is too good to wish or do his neighbor any harm. God will have no gossips as his guest. He does not keep company with verbal abusers. Those who are quick to express disapproval demonstrate a great lack of love. God is just, and therefore does not listen to hurtful lies, and we should not either. God is love. Therefore if he honors us by making us part of his family, let us not do anything that does not reflect that love. —*TNSDB*

I heard a sermon on, **"Wretched man that I am! Who will deliver me from this body of death?"** (Romans 7:24). And the preacher declared that Paul was not a Christian when he had that experience. Babe as I was, I knew better than to believe such an absurd statement. What besides divine grace could produce such a sighing and crying for deliverance from indwelling sin? I felt that a person who could talk such nonsense knew little of the life of a true believer. I said to myself, "What! Am I not alive because I feel a conflict within me? I never felt this fight when I was an unbeliever. When I was not a Christian I never groaned to be set free from sin. This battle is one of the surest proofs of my new birth, and yet this man cannot see it. He may be good for encouraging sinners, but he cannot feed believers."

—Sermon #1850 *Unlimited Love*

Christ's students never become wiser than the Bible.
The Holy Spirit is not given to replace the Scriptures,
but to equip us to understand and use them.

MARCH 1

It is a great blessing when the Lord removes the things that disturb the heart. Even curiosity may be a source of unrest. For many, curiosity is a great source of worry. I have sometimes wanted to know why the Lord does this and that with me. Blessed be his name, I am determined not to question him like that anymore. Somebody prayed the other day that I might see why the Lord has caused me to suffer lately. I hope the brother will not pray that anymore, because I do not want to know the Lord's reasons—why should I? I know that what he has done is right. I will not dishonor him by questioning him and wanting him to explain himself to a poor worm. —Sermon #1343 *The Jewel of Peace*

MARCH 2

Watch and pray that you may not enter into temptation. The spirit indeed is willing, but the flesh is weak. —Matthew 26:41

The danger of being trapped by sin is everywhere. On the land, on the sea, and in the air, there are evils all around. There are snares everywhere.

> Snares tuck your bed, and snares sit in your home;
> Snares watch your thoughts, and snares stick to your words;
> Snares in your quiet, snares in your commotion;
> Snares in your diet, snares in your devotion.

—*TNSDB* (Poem by Philip Quarles (a poet/theologian who lived during the 1600's).

The LORD said to Joshua [as he was preparing to enter the Promised Land]…

"This Book of the Law shall not depart from your mouth— *TALK ABOUT IT*

but you shall meditate on it day and night—*THINK ABOUT IT*

so that you may be careful to do according to all that is written in it—*PRACTICE IT.*

For then you will make your way prosperous, and then you will have good success—*REJOICE IN IT.*

Have I not commanded you? Be strong and courageous. Do not be frightened, and do not be dismayed, for the LORD your God is with you wherever you go." —Joshua 1:8-9

Where God's command is our authority we can afford to be bold. Who shall contradict us when the Lord of Hosts gives us clear direction? To be afraid, in such a case, is to dishonor our Invincible Commander. When the Lord is on their side, the believer has every reason to be confident. *—TNSDB*

Then Joshua rose early in the morning. —Joshua 3:1a

He did not serve God and his people in a lazy manner. He who wants to accomplish great things will never do them by lying in bed.

And they came to the Jordan, he and all the people of Israel, and lodged there before they passed over. —Joshua 3:2

They had a promise that they would cross over the Jordan River, but they did not know how it would be accomplished. Nevertheless they went forward in faith. If we only know our responsibility up to a certain point, let us continue to that point, even if we cannot see another inch beyond it. Let us follow God's directions as far as we know and leave what happens next to him.

—TNSDB

While the people of Israel were encamped at Gilgal, they kept the Passover on the fourteenth day of the month in the evening on the plains of Jericho. —Joshua 5:10

Before they began the conquest of Canaan the people focused their attention on circumcision and the Passover. We cannot expect God to help us if we are careless about keeping his commands. Before getting involved with any Christian activity it is best to look inwardly. When all is right within ourselves, then we shall be in a fit condition to do battle with the evils around us.

—TNSDB

And the day after the Passover, on the very day, they ate of the produce of the land, unleavened cakes and parched grain. And the manna ceased the day after they ate of the produce of the land. And there was no longer manna for the people of Israel, but they ate of the fruit of Canaan that year.

—Joshua 5:11-12

We must not expect miracles when ordinary circumstances will accomplish his will. There is, if we would only see it, as much wisdom and grace in supplying our daily needs by common methods as there would be in the Lord's raining bread from heaven on us. We may also mention here that God will continue to provide what we need until we receive our inheritance above. We must gather the manna of the wilderness until we feast upon the harvests of Immanuel's land. Grace will help us every day until we enter glory. *—TNSDB*

When Joshua was by Jericho, he lifted up his eyes and looked, and behold, a man was standing before him with his drawn sword in his hand. —Joshua 5:13

The Lord Jesus usually appears to his people in a way that proves his oneness with them. He shows himself to be like his brothers. To Abraham the pilgrim he appeared as a pilgrim. With Jacob the wrestler he wrestled. To Shadrach, Meshach and Abednego he appeared as one in the furnace. And to Joshua the soldier he showed himself as a warrior. Our Lord is the defender of his chosen and will show himself strong on their behalf. —*TNSDB*

"One Thing I Do." —Philippians 3:13

There is "one thing" that Paul speaks about; "One thing I do." Someone has said that the man who does one thing is a formidable opponent. I like to see those Christians who have a definite work and are doing it. I like to see them work in "the burden of the day and the scorching heat" and never weaken. I suppose it will turn out in this city as it has in many other places where we have been, where many, having received a new spirit, are asking what they shall do. They have been born again; and in that new life they are all full of soul, full of life, and a fire burns in their souls, and they want to declare the news of salvation.

The cry is, "What shall I do?" Let me say to you, find one thing and do it well. Do not think anything you do for the Lord is a little work. What seems like a little work to you may be the mightiest thing that has ever been done. You are a Sunday school teacher, for example, and have a class of little boys; you do not know what those boys may become. There may be a Martin Luther, there may be a George Whitefield, there may be a John Bunyan there. You may lead these little boys to Christ, and they may go out and move the world like Luther did. —D. L. Moody, *The Six "One Things"*

Her ways are of pleasantness; and all her paths are peace.

—Proverbs 3:17

In some cases, great happiness is not realized because known duties are neglected. The promise cannot enter because "sin is crouching at the door." Even an unknown duty may whip us with "a light beating," and a few lashes may greatly injure our happiness. Let us try to know the Lord's will in all things, and then let us obey it without a trace of hesitation. It is not about the path of our willfulness, but about the road of divine wisdom that we read, "Her ways are of pleasantness; and all her paths are peace."

—*According to Promise*

Men of the world whose portion is in this life. —Psalm 17:14

You have no reason to complain about having little, because everything that God has is yours. Whether in prosperity or adversity, life or death, everything is yours. What God gives is for your comfort. What he denies or takes away is to test you; it is for the increasing of those graces that are far more gracious than any temporary enjoyment. If you can see the wicked and ungodly swimming in wealth and ease, while you are forced to struggle to make ends meet, and have learned to have a holy contempt and disregard of the world, then believe it, God has given you more than if he had given you the world itself.

—Ezekiel Hopkins (1633-1690)

MARCH 11

God chose what is foolish in this world to shame the wise; God chose what is weak in the world to shame the strong; God chose what is low and despised in the world, even things that are not, to bring to nothing things that are, so that no human being might boast in the presence of God.

—1 Corinthians 1:27-29

God's election does not take human greatness into account. The preacher must not change his message just to keep from offending persons the world thinks are great. He is to proclaim his message to ordinary people and be satisfied if his converts are despised as being the worst humans on earth. If God's election was for the great, then he might have given them a philosophical gospel presented with highly intellectual speeches that most people could not understand. But this is not our Lord's gospel.

Let us hold tightly to the old gospel and love the honest pastors who care more about seeing sinners saved than about being thought of as great public speakers. The gospel which saved the apostles, the martyrs, the reformers, and our godly ancestors, is quite good enough for us. While others want to be wise according to worldly standards, we will follow the teaching of the Lord.

—TNSDB

MARCH 12

Blessed by the LORD ...with the choicest fruits of the sun and the rich yield of the months." —Deuteronomy 33:14

The sun brings growth and wealth over time. It takes time to develop spiritual maturity. *—TNSDB*

RELIANCE ON GOD AS OUR CHOSEN LIFE PRINCIPLE

If self-reliance can make a man, how much more can God-reliance! Relying on God is more justifiable, more humble, more certain, and more honoring. Our own powers can only reach so far and no further. We are tethered like a dog on a lease and cannot go beyond our limit. But the divine power is unlimited and unchangeable; the person who trusts God has a force at his back beyond all comparison. He will have no need to determine if he has the means to accomplish any goal he wisely sets; he may draw on the adequacy of God. The Greatest Power will prove great enough for us in all emergencies. God's power is established and unchanging; we may depend on it as long as eternity lasts. It is to our great advantage to place our reliance where we may increase it from day to day without any risk of too much confidence.

—*The Clue of the Maze*

Esau despised his birthright. —Genesis 25:34

Esau valued his birthright so little that a sorry bowl of stew was enough to buy it from him. Surely it was the most expensive dish of meat ever bought. Of course, we remember a little fruit that cost us much more. Many people who live for this world trade their souls for the pleasures of an hour. They cry, "Let us eat and drink, for tomorrow we die" (1 Corinthians 15:32). Many have thrown aside all hope of heaven for the hope of being rich, for the enjoyment of having pleasure, or just to have their own way. This is really trading pearls for pebbles, diamonds for fakes, and lasting happiness for short-lived amusement. May those who are still young take this sad act of Esau as a warning and eagerly choose that which will not be taken from them. —*TNSDB*

Now Sarai, Abram's wife, had borne him no children. She had a female Egyptian servant whose name was Hagar.

—Genesis 16:1

Sarai therefore suggested to Abram that Hagar should become his secondary wife. This was a very usual custom in those days, but it was not a praiseworthy one. It was an act of unbelief for Sarai to suggest it. It is not always easy to wait patiently for the Lord's time. We all tend to be too quick to run to our own methods; as if the Lord needed our help to fulfill his promises.

—*TNSDB*

And Abram listened to the voice of Sarai. —Genesis 16:2

Those we love best may be the means of leading us astray. Adam, the father of mankind, sinned by listening to his spouse and now the father of the faithful follows his poor example.

And when Hagar saw that she had conceived, she looked with contempt on her mistress. And Sarai said to Abram, "May the wrong done to me be on you! I gave my servant to your embrace, and when she saw that she had conceived, she looked on me with contempt. May the LORD judge between you and me!" —Genesis 16:4-5

It was Sarai who suggested doing this and now she blames her husband for it. It is no use to blame others for our mistakes. If we turn off the road of correctness, we shall certainly and personally feel the pain for it. —*TNSDB*

MARCH 17

And Hagar bore Abram a son, and Abram called the name of his son, whom Hagar bore, Ishmael. —Genesis 16:15

But Ishmael was not, as he had hoped, the promised heir. On the contrary, he became the cause of many trials to the family. When we look to the world to help grace, or reason to assist faith, we fail to reach our goal. Instead, we guarantee sorrow. This whole scene is a painful one. It should warn us that even in good families sin may cause infighting and bring unhappiness and heartache.

—TNSDB

Beware of trusting yourself even when you are in your best state of mind. Self is as fickle as the wind that constantly changes direction.

MARCH 18

**I am a sojourner on the earth;
hide not your commandments from me!**

—Psalm 119:19

Lord, to the world I am a stranger. Do not let me be a stranger to your will. If I use your commandments as my map, I will find the road to heaven, even while traveling in this foreign country we call the world. Without your commandments, I will be like a traveler lost in the desert.

Your testimonies are my delight; they are my counselors.

—Psalm 119:24

As a result of meditating in the word, David was kept from both sadness and confusion. We can only get comfort from the Bible by following its directions and living by its instructions.

—TNSDB

MARCH 19

When he appears we shall be like him. —1 John 3:2

We are not what we would be; but then we are not what we shall be. Our progress is slow; but it is certain progress. The end is secured by all-powerful grace. It is right that we are not satisfied with ourselves, yet this holy restlessness should not rob us of our perfect peace in Christ Jesus. If the Lord is at rest with us, will we not have rest in him? —Sermon #1990 *A Sermon for the Present Time*

---

*We are not able to think or say anything
properly without God guiding us.*

MARCH 20

It is better to be of a lowly spirit with the poor than to divide the spoil with the proud. —Proverbs 16:19

This may not seem like good advice, and few would choose to follow it, but the Word of God knows best. The person dividing up the loot is afraid that he may lose it again, and is probably already unhappy with his share and greedy for more. But the humble mind is satisfied, and therefore possesses happiness.

—*TNSDB*

**Be not among…gluttonous eaters of meat,
for…the glutton will come to poverty.** —Proverbs 23:20

Gluttonous eaters of meat do not fear God. They feast "without fear" (Jude 12). Gluttony is a sin to which few pay attention and those who indulge in it rarely repent of it. Yet, it is offensive to God and the practice of it demonstrates a lack of the fear of God in the heart. It is so disagreeable that God forbids his people to be in the company of those who are gluttonous. He also tells us these kinds of people are blots and blemishes on those who keep company with them. They do not fear God (2 Peter 2:13; Romans 13:13; 1 Peter 4:4). —John Bunyan, *The Fear of God*

LUKEWARMNESS

Brothers and sisters, we need more earnestness in the Sunday school, with the person who distributes tracts, and even with private Christians living their lives, reading their Bibles, praying, attending worship services, and quietly going about doing good. Lukewarmness in religion is always to be loathed and deserted, because it is a shameful and glaring inconsistency. I would not have you even distributing tracts with a lukewarm heart. I would not have you dare to visit the sick unless your heart is filled with love to Christ. Either do such work well, or do not do it at all.

—Sermon #2802 *Lukewarmness*

MARCH 23

And David inquired of the LORD, "Shall I go up against the Philistines? Will you give them into my hand?" And the LORD said to David, "Go up, for I will certainly give the Philistines into your hand." —2 Samuel 5:19

David's path seemed obvious, but he wanted God to lead in every step he took. No one ever lost his way by asking for directions too many times. Asking the Lord to direct us is never unnecessary. We should all follow David's example. If we do, we will walk in the way of peace all our days. —*TNSDB*

MARCH 24

You have tried my heart, you have visited me by night.
—Psalm 17:3

Like Peter, David uses the argument, "Lord, you know everything; you know that I love you" (John 21:17). It is a most assuring thing to be able to appeal immediately to the Lord, and call upon our Judge to be a witness for our defense. "Beloved, if our heart does not condemn us, we have confidence before God" (1 John 3:21). David said, "You have visited me in the night."— "Lord you have entered my house at all hours. You have seen me when no one else is around. You have come in when I was not aware of your presence. You have noted what I did in private. You know whether I am guilty of the crimes that I am accused of committing." Happy is the person who can remember that God sees everything, is always present with us and still find comfort in knowing it. We also have had our midnight visits from our Lord and they have been very sweet. So wonderful, in fact, that just thinking about them makes us want more of these visits. Lord, if we really were hypocrites, could we have had such marvelous fellowship with you or hungered for more of them? —*TNSDB*

We walk by faith, not by sight. —2 Corinthians 5:7

Those promises that are yet unfulfilled are precious helps to our advancement in the spiritual life. We are encouraged by extremely great and precious promises to set our heart on higher things. The expectation of good things to come strengthens us to endure and keep moving forward. You and I are like little children who are learning to walk, and are coaxed to take step after step by a treat being held out to them. We are persuaded to try the trembling legs of our faith by the sight of a promise. As a result we are drawn to go a step nearer to our God. —*According to Promise*

The great love of Jesus is understood best when his redeemed ones show it in their lives, at all times and in all places.

MARCH 26

For I am not ashamed of the gospel, for it is the power of God for salvation to everyone who believes. —Romans 1:16

You have no reason to despair. If the ministers of Christ will only come back to preaching the gospel of Jesus Christ, plainly, simply, and with the Holy Spirit sent down from heaven, we will drive those who would replace the gospel with rituals or entertainment back to where they came, as our fathers did before us. Never lose your faith in the gospel. Always believe that our power is gone when we get away from the cross. But also believe this: When we come back to the truth as it is in Jesus, God glorifies his name.

—Sermon #909 *Voices From the Excellent Glory*

MR. LAW AND MR. GRACE

Here is a boy in school, and the teacher's name is Mr. Law. He holds his rod over him and says, in a cold, severe tone, "You shall not do this, and you shall not do that." This went on for some time, and there was no love or affection between the boy and his teacher. But by-and-by the principal comes and takes the student out of that room and puts him in another class, this one taught by Mr. Grace. The boy, you see, can't be in both rooms at the same time— can't have both teachers at the same time. Now, we are not under law, but under grace, and all the Lord wants is to deal in grace, and bring us out from the curse of the law. He wants to include everyone in love. —D. L. Moody, *Abounding Grace*

"Aha, Aha! Our eyes have seen it!" —Psalm 35:21

What is more common than for the wickedest sinners to use the worst behavior of God's dearest saints as their excuse and authorization to do the same? Thus the alcoholic sees holy Noah as a drinking companion, and sees his nakedness more than Ham ever did. In the same way, the one who indulges their impure appetites quotes David and points him out as the supporter of his immorality. Certainly, if there is any grief that can overshadow the perfect joys of the saints in heaven, it is that their names and examples should be brought up by wicked and sinful people, to support their grossest sins and wickedness, to the great dishonor of God. But let these people know, that God has raised up these people in his church to be reminders of his mercy, and to declare to humble and repentant sinners that he can pardon even such great sins. Yet if any, as a result of this, use these as excuses to sin, instead of seeing them as monuments of God's mercy, God will establish them as pillars of salt. —Ezekiel Hopkins (1633-1690)

Many are the sorrows of the wicked,
but steadfast love surrounds the one who trusts in the
LORD.
Be glad in the LORD, and rejoice, O righteous,
and shout for joy, all you upright in heart!

—Psalm 32:10-11

Those who begin with holy weeping shall end with holy rejoicing. If there is someone reading this who is unforgiven, let him or her go to the heavenly Father and cry for that gracious forgiveness that is given to all who believe in Jesus. It is not given as a reward for good works. It is not given because of any efforts of our own. It is the free gift of God in Christ Jesus. Paul says that David is describing "the blessing of the one to whom God counts righteousness apart from works" (Romans 4:6). The apostle clearly says that our salvation is not a matter of merit but of grace. The very worst and most horrible sins will be freely and immediately forgiven if we will confess them to the Lord and trust in the infinite worthiness of his dear Son. Do not wait! Rush, right now, to the open fountain of Jesus' blood. —*TNSDB*

MARCH 30

You have seen O LORD; be not silent! O Lord, be not far from me! —Psalm 35:22

Here is comfort. Our heavenly Father knows all our sorrow. Omniscience is the saint's light that never goes out. A father will not tolerate his child being abused for long. Will God not avenge his own elect? Oh Lord, rebuke those who are your enemies and mine. A word will do it. Clear my character, comfort my heart. Walk with me in the fiery furnace. Stand beside me when I am publicly attacked. The sweet presence of God is the divine comfort of the persecuted; his painful absence would be their greatest misery. —*The Treasury of David*

**And let the net that he hid ensnare him; let him fall into it—
to his destruction!** —Psalm 35:8

Who would not approve of Goliath being slain with his own
sword? Who would not applaud when proud Haman placed
Mordecai on the king's horse and proclaimed the king's delight in
him. The wicked will be ruined by their own devices; all the
arrows they shoot at the righteous will land on their own heads.
Maxentius built a false bridge to drown Constantine, but was
drowned himself. Henry the Third of France was stabbed in the
very same room where he helped bring about the cruel massacre
of the French Protestants. It is common with God to catch
persecutors in the same traps and pits that they have prepared for
his people, as many thousands in this nation have experienced.
Today, many are setting traps and digging pits for the righteous—
who would rather burn in the fiery furnace than bow to their Baal.
Wait and weep, saints, and weep and wait a little longer, and you
will see that the Lord will trap them in their own traps, and cause
them to fall into their own pits—the ones they dug for you.

—Condensed from Thomas Brooks (1608-1680)

APRIL 1

GUARANTEED

Jesus is the Guarantee of the promises. He who did not spare his own Son will deny nothing to his people. If he had ever thought of taking back a promise, he would have done it before he had made the infinite sacrifice of his Only Son. There can never be any suspicion about the Lord revoking any one of the promises since he has already fulfilled the greatest and most costly of them all. "How will he not also with him graciously give us all things?" (Romans 8:32). —*According to Promise*

APRIL 2

We have a building from God, a house not made with hands.

—2 Corinthians 5:1

The ambitions of man have been defeated, but not the goals of God. The promises of man may be broken—many of them are made to be broken—but the promises of God will all be fulfilled. He is a promise maker, but he never was a promise breaker. He is a promise keeping God, and every one of his people shall prove it. This is my grateful, personal confidence, "The Lord will fulfill his purpose for me"—unworthy me, lost and ruined me. He will save me; and—I, among the blood-washed throng, shall wave the palm, and wear the crown. And shout loud victory. I go to a land that is untouched by the plows of earth, where it is greener than this world's best pastures, and richer than her most productive fields. I go to a building of more splendid architecture than man has ever built. It is not of mortal design. It is "a house not made with hands, eternal in the heavens." Everything I will know and enjoy in heaven, will be given to me by the Lord; and I will say, when I at last appear before him— "Grace all the work shall crown through everlasting days; it lays in heaven the topmost stone, and well deserves the praise." —*A Defense of Calvinism*

APRIL 3

"I will bow down…in the fear of you." —Psalm 5:7

God expects us to serve him with fear and trembling. It is offensive for a man to be in the presence, or in the service, of his prince, and behave in a careless manner. He is expected to exercise proper respect, that is, fear, for the majesty of his lord when he is in his presence or carrying out his business. And if this is so, how can service to God be accepted by him if it is done without the fear of him? This disrespect must be highly offensive to God and those who serve in that way must be rebuked.

—John Bunyan, *The Fear of God*

APRIL 4

And when they came to the threshing floor of Chidon, Uzzah put out his hand to take hold of the ark, for the oxen stumbled. And the anger of the LORD was kindled against Uzzah, and he struck him down because he put out his hand to the ark, and he died there before God. —1 Chronicles 13:9-10

There are very many today who commit the sin of Uzzah. They dream that Christianity will suffer greatly unless they adapt it to the tastes and whims of their generation. They change its teachings. They decorate its worship to satisfy modern desires. They add philosophy to the simple gospel. Plain speaking must give place to eloquence. In their zeal and conceit they attempt to help HIM who does not need such helpers. They insult the true religion their unbelieving fear tries to protect. We must beware of even imagining that our hand is needed to steady God's ark. The thought is blasphemy. —*TNSDB*

Men of the world whose portion is in this life. —Psalm 17:4

God gives men of the world a portion in this life to show them what little value there is in all these things, and to show the world what little value there is in all the things that are here below. Certainly if they were much good they would never have them. It can be argued that it is no outstanding feature to be physically strong, because an ox has more strength than you. It can be argued that being extremely agile is no big deal, because a dog is more agile than you. It can be argued that fancy clothes are not important, because a peacock is better adorned than you. It can be argued that gold and silver are not all that valuable, because those living in India, who do not know God, have more than you. It must be argued that if these things had any great worth in them, then God would certainly never have given them to men of the world.

—Jeremiah Burroughs (1600-1646)

NOW!

Prepare *now*. Do not wait a month before starting, but begin now! It is often the word that saves sinners, and it is the word that brings life and energy to Christians. Who can tell how many souls "tomorrow" has destroyed. "Tomorrow" devours souls like the grave devours the dead. That demon word *tomorrow* has caused great sorrow. And who can tell how many Christian churches have been kept from growing by the policy that said, "Wait a little"? Out with such horrible advice! Wait? Impossible! Death does not wait! Hell does not pause! Sin does not take a vacation from its mad career! If the devil, and death, and hell would wait, then we might have an excuse for standing around doing nothing; but until then, our motto must be, "Forward!" Now, my brothers and sisters; prepare for the blessing right now. God is ready to give the blessing when we are ready to receive it.

—Sermon #747 *Make This Valley Full of Trenches*

HALLELUJAH!

They hanged our Lord on a tree; they took his body down and buried it in a tomb cut in stone; and they set their seal on the rock that was rolled to the entrance of the tomb. Surely that was the end of the Christ and his cause.

Boast not, you priests and Pharisees! Your guard over the stone and seal is useless! Your dreams have not come true. When the appointed time had come, the living Christ came forth. The cords of death could not hold him. "He who sits in the heavens laughs; the Lord holds them in derision" (Psalm 2:4). The outcome of the battle is not in doubt. The end of the conflict is sure and certain. Even now, I think I hear the shout, "Hallelujah! For the Lord our God the Almighty reigns."

—Sermon #1990 *A Sermon for the Present Time*

The wicked will come together for evil, but Christians often refuse to come together for good. This is very shameful.

THE PROMISED LAND

When our inner joys lift us high, and cause us to break out in song, we are hearing the preludes of the heavenly hallelujahs. If we desire to taste the grapes of Canaan, behold, they are brought to us by those emotions and anticipations, that, under the guidance of the Spirit, have gone, like spies into the Promised Land, and brought back its finest fruits. —*According to Promise*

APRIL 9

WHEN ZERAH THE ETHIOPIAN CAME OUT AGAINST KING ASA

And Asa cried to the LORD his God, "O LORD, there is none like you to help, between the mighty and the weak. Help us, O LORD our God, for we rely on you, and in your name we have come against this multitude. O LORD, you are our God; let not man prevail against you." —2 Chronicles 14:11

This is a great example of the prayer of faith. The million soldiers of Zerah are not enough to shake Asa's faith. He knows they are nothing before the Lord and does not fear their large number. He is not discouraged because his army is not as strong as Zerah's. He knows the Lord is all powerful and does not depend on the strength of his people. It is a glorious thing to be able to call on the Lord our God and then to rest in him without concern or fear; knowing that our cause is safe because it is about the Lord's honor and it is in his own hands. Let us follow Asa's example. Let us trust God and not be afraid when we encounter great trails and difficulties. —*TNSDB*

APRIL 10

But you, take courage! Do not let your hands be weak, for your work shall be rewarded. —2 Chronicles 15:7

Israel's history was clear. When they were faithful to God they prospered, when they turned their backs on him he did not bless them. They made or unmade their own fortunes. Have we not also learned by this time that we are happy when we live near to God and miserable when we fall back into our old evil habits? Let us not forget this remarkable truth. —*TNSDB*

Friendship with the world is enmity with God. —James 4:4

One group says, "I don't know whether I love God or not. I am really anxious to know whether or not I love God." Now, if you are really anxious it won't take you long to find out. You cannot love God and the world at the same time, because they abhor each other. They are at enmity, always have been and always will be. It is the world that crucified God's Son; it was the world that put God's Son to death. Therefore, if we love the world it is a pretty good proof that the love of the Father is not in us. We may say our prayers and go through some religious exercises, but our hearts are not right with God because we cannot love God and the world at the same time. We have to get the world under our feet and the love of God must be first in our hearts or else we have not got the love of God. —D. L. Moody, *Christian Love*

Honor everyone. Love the brotherhood.

Fear God. Honor the emperor. —1 Peter 2:17

Four general principles that are intended to balance one another. There should be a blending of all of them in our lives. We are to honor not only our country's leaders, but everyone. Every human being should be treated with respect. Not just rich people or those who always wear the latest style, or who are admired by the world, but poor people and those who wear secondhand clothing and do not seem to have friends. We are all created in the image of God and we should treat everyone in the best way we can. —*TNSDB*

Commit your work to the LORD, and your plans will be established. —Proverbs 16:3

Both our physical and spiritual concerns will be safe when we place them in the Lord's hands. Then the peace that comes from our faith, will give us a steady, calm, determined, and joyful state of mind.

The LORD has made everything for its purpose, even the wicked for the day of trouble. —Proverbs 16:4

Let the wicked oppose God all they want; he will make them serve some part in his plans.

When a man's ways please the LORD, he makes even his enemies to be at peace with him. —Proverbs 16:7

The Lord often does this, as in the cases of Isaac and Abimelech, Jacob and Esau. But this truth must be qualified by another truth. The Lord's enemies will not always be at peace with us, no matter how kind and pleasant we may be. —*TNSDB*

How much better to get wisdom than gold!
To get understanding is to be chosen rather than silver.
—Proverbs 16:16

Wisdom from God is better, much better than gold. No one can even imagine how much better. Gold can be earned by anyone, but only God can chose us, by his free grace, to be a part of his holy family. Gold is just a valuable piece of earth, but grace is the very heart of heaven. Gold is soon spent and gone. The more we use grace, the more grace we are given. Gold may be stolen from us, but no one can take grace away from us. Gold and silver cannot comfort us in death, but true wisdom can. The wealth of precious metals will be useless in eternity, but grace will make us glorious there. Lord, always give us understanding through your Holy Spirit! —*TNSDB*

For God alone my soul waits in silence; from him comes my salvation. —Psalm 62:1

Our salvation comes to us only from the Lord. Therefore we should wait on or depend on him alone. If depending on God is worship, then depending on anything in creation is idolatry. If depending on God only is true faith, then thinking we need others to help us is reckless unbelief. Very few of us avoid this evil way of thinking and really depend on God only. —*TNSDB*

He only is my rock and my salvation,
my fortress; I shall not be shaken.
On God rests my salvation and my glory;
my mighty rock, my refuge is God. —Psalm 62:6-7

Notice how David brands his own initials on every title he gives to God. He rejoices in my hope, my rock, my salvation, my glory, and so on. There are seven my's in two verses and there can never be too many. The faith that applies divine blessings personally is the faith we all need.

Trust in him at all times, O people;
pour out your heart before him;
God is a refuge for us. *Selah.* —Psalm 62:8

God has shown the fullness of his love to us. We should show our emptiness to him. Turn your soul upside down in his presence and let your innermost thoughts, desires, sorrows and sins be poured out like water. To keep our misery to our self just increases our hopelessness. The end of our deep distress is close when we freely acknowledge it to the Lord. —*TNSDB*

Selah. —The Psalms

This is a musical pause, the precise meaning of which is not known. Some think it is simply a rest, a pause in the music. Others say it means, "Lift up the tune—sing louder—raise the tune to a higher key—there is more important matter to come, therefore retune your harps." Harp-strings quickly get out of tune and need to be tightened again to their proper sound; and our heart-strings are certainly and constantly getting out of tune. Let "*Selah*" teach us to pray,

> "Oh may my heart in tune be found
> Like David's harp of solemn sound."

At least, we may learn that wherever we see "*Selah*," we should look on it as a note to be more observant. Let us read the passage that precedes or follows it with greater earnestness, for surely there is always something excellent where we are required to rest and pause and mediate, or when we are required to lift up our hearts in grateful song. —*The Treasury of David*

Put no trust in extortion;
set no vain hopes on robbery;
if riches increase, set not your heart on them.

—Psalm 62:10

This is a difficult rule. Worldly wealth is a slimy thing and is too likely to stick to the heart. Maybe this is why so many of the saints are poor. Perhaps the Lord is protecting them from being tempted by growing riches. Our hope must be in God alone. Placing our confidence in the treasures of this life is as hopeless as trying to bottle the wind. —*TNSDB*

We walk by faith, not by sight. —2 Corinthians 5:7

The blind man is as well off in the darkness as those who have their eyes. In fact, his habit of finding his way in the dark makes him the better of the two. Therefore, if faith teaches us to take the path where the end is not obvious to human eyes, we will be better prepared for that land which the mortal eye has not seen. This much is certain, if we follow God by faith, then we do not need to be distressed because of his apparent absence and his actual invisibility. The dog, that hunts by scent, does not need to see its quarry and the person who follows the path of obedience by faith has no need to seek for signs and tangible guarantees, because faith supplies him or her with a more certain sense.

—The Clue of the Maze

Trusting in God is the duty and privilege of all saints,
at all times, in all places.

All his thoughts are, "There is no God" —Psalm 10:4b

The only place where God is not is in the thoughts of the wicked. This is a damning accusation; because where the God of heaven is not, the lord of hell is reigning and raging. If God is not in our thoughts, our thoughts will bring us to damnation.

—The Treasury of David

SEEING FOR ONE'S SELF

We are not being too strict when we demand that every honest person should read the Bible personally. In testing a Book that claims to be the revelation of God's mind, we would not be treating it with proper respect if we trust to others' opinions, no matter who they are. Secondhand information lacks assurance and clarity. A personal investigation is far more acceptable and useful.

Does our "wisdom" decide a matter before it hears it? Is there any reason the Scriptures should not be studied thoroughly? It is part of being a wise person to calmly and seriously search those famous writings which are prized by so many brilliant minds. The voice that cried to Augustine, "Take up and read," was no sound of folly. To take up and read a great and good book cannot be to our harm. —*The Clue of the Maze*

You have been the helper of the fatherless. —Psalm 10:14

God exercises a more special providence over people in desperate circumstances; and therefore among his other titles is this one, to be a *"helper of the fatherless."* Now what greater comfort is there than this, that there is one who governs the world who is so wise he cannot be mistaken, so faithful he cannot deceive, so full of pity he cannot neglect his people, and so powerful that he can make even stones turn into bread if he please! God does not rule the world only as an absolute monarch, but by his wisdom and goodness as a tender father. His greatest pleasure is not showing his sovereign power, or his incredible wisdom, but his enormous goodness, to which he makes his other attributes secondary. —Stephen Charnock (1628-1680)

For each will have to bear his own load. —Galatians 6:5

Each of us has his own load of responsibility to deal with. Therefore we would do well to remember our own faults and sympathize with the faults of others. When we are tempted to condemn others, we should consider our own failings. —*TNSDB*

If many of those people who are now called homeless would go to work, we would all have sympathy for them. – D. L. Moody The Prodigal Son

---

PRAYING IN A BUSINESSLIKE WAY

The precious promises of God are clearly intended to be taken to him, and exchanged for the blessings that they guarantee. Prayer takes the promise to the Bank of Faith, and receives the golden blessing. Pay attention to how you pray. Do it in a businesslike way. Never make prayer a dead formality. Some people pray a long time, but do not get what they are supposed to ask for, because they do not plead the promise in a truthful, businesslike way.

If you were to go into a bank, and stand for an hour talking to the teller, and then come out again without your cash, what good would that do you? If I go to a bank, I pass my check across the counter, take my money, and go about my business; that is the best way to pray. Ask for what you want, because the Lord has promised it. Believe that you have the blessing, and go on about your business in full assurance of the promise. Rise from your knees singing, because the promise is fulfilled; and as a result your prayer will be answered. It is not the length of your prayer, but the strength of your prayer that wins with God; and the strength of prayer lies in your faith in the promise that you have pleaded before the Lord. —*According to Promise*

He found him in a desert land, and in the howling waste of the wilderness; he encircled him, he cared for him, he kept him as the apple of his eye. —Deuteronomy 32:10

There is an organization in London where they take in poor little homeless children. They take them in and the first thing they do is have their picture taken, just as they look when they find them, in their rags and dirt. Then after they have grown up there, and have had all the benefit of the organization, before they go, they have their photograph taken again; and they give them the two photographs. One is to show them how they looked when they came to them, and the other, that they may compare them. It would be a good thing if we could remember ourselves distinctly as we were when the Lord first found us, and compare it with ourselves when he leaves us on the hilltops of glory.

—D. L. Moody, *Message to Young Converts*

Where your treasure is, there your heart will be also.
—Matthew 6:21

Whatever we choose to be our treasure will be sure to be what pulls at our heart. If our goal is to pile up earthly riches, our hearts will, step-by-step, make money the most important thing in our lives. On the other hand, if our most treasured possessions are heavenly things, our hearts will rise to a higher and more spiritual state. The condition of the heart is certain to be affected by what kind of treasure we store up. Will the children of God give their hearts away to passing joys, that will be destroyed or stolen?

—*TNSDB*

APRIL 27

Many believed in his name when they saw the signs that he was doing. But Jesus on his part did not entrust himself to them, because he knew all people. —John 2:23-24

The gospel wins many converts, but over time it becomes clear that not all of them understood and were sincere. This did not surprise Jesus and it should not surprise us. Verse twenty-four tells us that he did not trust those who were so eager to claim their loyalty to him. Jesus understood the fickleness of human hearts, the superficial nature of that which often passes for true religion, and the ease with which hasty conversions are turned into sudden and final apostasies. May the Lord cleanse our hearts and keep us to the end. —*TNSDB*

APRIL 28

Let everyone who names the name of the Lord depart from iniquity. —2 Timothy 2:19

We should always have a reverent awe of God on our hearts anytime we think about him, or hear his name, but most of all, when we speak his name. This should be especially the case in preaching, praying, and when God is the subject of our conversation. I do not mention only these to make any excuse for using his name lightly at anytime. We should always use it with reverence and godly fear. But I say it to remind Christians that they should not use the name of Lord in a light or pointless way when fulfilling religious responsibilities.

—John Bunyan, *The Fear of God*

FAITH IS ALWAYS AT WORK

Sincere faith is not found in the tribe of the lazy and irresponsible. To attempt nothing and leave all things to chance is something that breeds despair rather than confidence. Convinced of the richness of the soil, the farmer sows it; assured of victory, the soldier fights for it; confident in his good ship, the mariner puts out to sea. We cannot believe in God, who is always working, and then stop working ourselves. Faith never considers it advantageous to rust in shameful idleness. No, in matters of everyday living, faith tunnels through the Alps, joins the seas, invades the unknown, and braves the hazardous. When we believe the most, we accomplish the most. It becomes a matter of the greatest importance that we not only have faith, but that we have it "more abundantly." The rule of the kingdom is, "According to your faith be it done to you" (Matthew 9:29). —*The Clue of the Maze*

He has granted to us his precious and very great promises.
—2 Peter 1:4

If the promises are this great and precious, then let us accept them with joy and believe them. Will I urge the children of God to do this? No, I will not dishonor them like that; surely they will believe their own Father! Surely, surely, it ought to be the easiest thing in the world for the sons and daughters of the Most High to believe in him who has given them "the right to become children of God!" My brothers and sisters, do not begin to doubt the promise by not believing, but believe up to the hilt!

—*According to Promise*

MAY 1

But when you give to the needy, do not let your left hand know what your right hand is doing, so that your giving may be in secret. And your Father who sees in secret will reward you. —Matthew 6:3-4

Do not let what you have done become so known that it goes to your head. Do not keep counting what you have given like a miser keeps counting his money. Instead, go and give even more. Those who are anxious about having their donations publicly acknowledged, will give nothing unless it is put down on a printed list for all to see. They should take warning from our Lord's words. Believers should also learn to give to the cause of God and to the poor in the quietest manner possible. —*TNSDB*

MAY 2

Rejoice that your names are written in heaven. —Luke 10:20

I do not know what you will discover to comfort *you*, but there is nothing but this doctrine of election that satisfies me, nothing but this will give me any comfort. This teaching has sometimes filled our souls with joy that we hardly knew how to contain. We have mounted "up with wings like eagles," up to our God, who has caused us to rejoice in him because of his distinguishing favor. What caused David to leap and dance before the ark of the covenant? The doctrine of election; for what did he say to the woman who despised him for dancing? He said, "It was before the Lord, who chose me above your father." That truth moved him to excitement and joy; and many heirs of heaven have danced before God's ark when the Spirit has shown them that their names are included among the chosen ones of Jehovah.

—Sermon #324 *Effects of Sound Doctrine*

WHEN JESUS WALKED ON WATER

The boat by this time was a long way from land, beaten by the waves, for the wind was against them. And in the fourth watch of the night he came to them, walking on the sea.

—Matthew 14:24-25

In the first storm (Matthew 8:23-27) Jesus was in the ship with them; and so they must have felt all along that if things got worse, they could wake him up. The mere fact that he was physically there must have given them a sense of relative security. But Jesus does not want them to depend only on his bodily presence. They must not be like ivy that always needs an outward support. They must be like strong trees in the forest that withstand the strong blasts of the wind. So this time he puts them forth into the danger alone, just as a loving mother-bird thrusts her fledglings from the nest, that they may find their own wings and learn to use them. By doing this the Lord will awaken in them a confidence in his ever-ready help. They could never have imagined that Jesus could walk on the sea and may easily have lost hope that help would ever reach them. Yet the Lord does not fail them. When he has tested them to the uttermost, "In the fourth watch of the night," he appears beside them. In this way he teaches them a lesson for the rest of their lives: In all the coming storms of temptation, he is near them. Even though he may not always be seen by their bodily eyes, and however cut off from his help they may seem to be, yet he is indeed a very present help in trouble.

—R. C. Trench (1807-1886) *Parables of Our Lord*

If anyone would come after me, let him deny himself and take up his cross and follow me. —Mark 8:34

Those who are pulled from their respect of and obedience to the Word of God, by the pleasures or threats of men, stand condemned already. There are some who will certainly acknowledge the authority of the Word, but refuse to lower themselves to obey it.

Whatever they think of themselves, Christ declares that they are ashamed of the Word and condemned along with the others. "For whoever," he says, "is ashamed of me and of my words in this adulterous and sinful generation, of him will the Son of Man also be ashamed when he comes in the glory of his Father with the holy angels" (Mark 8:38). —John Bunyan, *The Fear of God*

MAY 5

Truly, truly, I say to you, whoever believes has eternal life.
—John 6:47

This plain and unlimited statement from the mouth of Jesus himself should greatly encourage and comfort all who believe. Do you trust in him alone? Then you have life, life that can never die, life that will be fully developed in eternal happiness. Do you feel that you do not have everlasting life? Nevertheless, if you are trusting in Jesus, the fact is undeniable and you certainly possess eternal life. Whatever your feelings may be, Jesus knows what he says, and his words are true. Believe it because he says so. What better reason can you ask for? —*TNSDB*

MAY 6

And rising very early in the morning, while it was still dark, he departed and went out to a desolate place, and there he prayed. —Mark 1:35

The Sun of Righteousness was up before the sun. How much must our Lord have loved prayer to give up his needed sleep, to spend time talking with his heavenly Father. He was sinless and yet needed to pray. Therefore, far be it from us to dream that we can do without it. Like our Lord, we must spend time in private to prepare ourselves for the public battle of life. —*TNSDB*

Then David said in his heart, "Now I shall perish one day by the hand of Saul." —1 Samuel 27:1a

Brothers and sisters in Christ, your case is similar—at least mine is. Oh Lord God! you have not left us at any time. We have had dark nights, but the star of your love has shined in the blackness. We have had our cloudy days, but have received glimpses of the sunlight of heaven. We have gone through many trials, but always to our gain, never to our loss. The conclusion from our past experience—at least, I can speak positively about my own—is, that he who has been with us in six troubles, will not leave us in the seventh. He has said, "I will never, never leave you, nor ever, ever, ever forsake you" (Hebrews 13:5). I repeat the text just as I find it in the Greek. What we have known about our faithful God, goes to show that he will keep us to the end; he will be our helper to the last. —Sermon #439 *The Danger of Doubting*

And the LORD said to [to the man clothed in linen, who had the writing case at his waist], "Pass through the city, through Jerusalem, and put a mark on the foreheads of the men who sigh and groan over all the abominations that are committed in [the house of the LORD]." —Ezekiel 9:4

Our great High Priest keeps the book of life and protects his own. No evil will touch them. Our Great Shepherd is the best qualified person to watch over his sheep, because he "knows who are his" (2 Timothy 2:19). The pen of mercy keeps a careful record and stands superior to the sword of vengeance. Repentance is the special mark of grace on the foreheads of those who truly love the Lord. Those who sigh and groan because of sin will live. —*TNSDB*

> "At that time I will bring you in,
>   at the time when I gather you together;
> for I will make you renowned and praised
>   among all the peoples of the earth,
> when I restore your fortunes
>   before your eyes," says the LORD. —Zephaniah 3:20

Persecution and contempt will end. In the latter days the saints will be honored for their excellence. Shame and disapproval is the cross that Christians must now carry for their Lord's sake, but the loving providence of God will change all this before long. Our enemies will be bewildered and our God will be glorified. Let us rest in the love of God and quietly wait for that great day. —*TNSDB*

My salvation will be forever, and my righteousness will never be dismayed. —Isaiah 51:6

God is faithful and will be true to his covenant. His is not a promise to be kept for only a few days or even a few years. His promises are forever. The Lord's promise of salvation will not be hidden in some far off corner; it will be proclaimed far and wide. Nothing can be more delightful than to possess this salvation and understand that this covenant of grace is built on a foundation that cannot be destroyed. —*TNSDB*

But concerning that day and hour no one knows, not even the angels of heaven, nor the Son, but the Father only.

—Matthew 24:36

The Thessalonians said, Christ is coming, therefore the day of the Lord *must be* in the very near future. They belonged to the class of fanatics who are always raving about "the signs of the times." They were like those who pretend to know what will happen within the next twenty years. There were impostors like that in Paul's day and there are impostors like that now. Do not believe them. They cannot see the future anymore than blind horses. Whether preachers or writers, I put them all down under the heading of impostors; because no one knows the future and no one can tell others about it. I care no more for their explanations of prophecy than for the pretended weeping eyes in statues of Mary. Yet they will continue their acts of dishonesty; one will say this, and another that, that this wonder will happen and that wonder will happen; and that terrible judgments will overwhelm our nation.

—Sermon #1850 *Unlimited Love*

And the ransomed of the LORD shall return
 and come to Zion with singing;
everlasting joy shall be upon their heads;
 they shall obtain gladness and joy,
 and sorrow and sighing shall flee away. —Isaiah 35:10

Zion is the end of our holy journey. It ends in happiness and singing that knows no end. Crowns of joy will be placed on the heads of all who follow the Lamb of God. Their mourning will be over. They will be with the Lord forever more. Many or our friends and relatives are among the happy travelers who have already arrived in heaven. We look forward to joining them at the end of the pathway of faith. —*TNSDB*

WHEN THE PEOPLE ASKED KING REHOBOAM
TO LIGHTEN THE HARD SERVICE OF HIS FATHER
—2 Chronicles 9:1-19

Lowering our expectations will often win over those who oppose our ideas. To give in a little in order to gain much is wise policy. The people had a right to what they asked. If the young prince would have agreed to their demands with a graceful spirit, he would have been the beloved ruler of an enthusiastic people.

—TNSDB

Dead flies make the perfumer's ointment give off a stench; so a little folly outweighs wisdom and honor. —Ecclesiastes 10:1

No matter how beautiful the jar or how excellent the fragrance, dead flies will destroy the precious lotion. And even so, what seem like unimportant faults will spoil a fine character. Being rude, having a short temper, making jokes about serious matters, unwillingness to give or spend money, self-centeredness, and a thousand other harmful flies have often turned the wonderful perfume of a Christian's life into a destructive odor to those who were around him. Let us pray for grace to avoid the smaller errors, so that they will not do serious harm to us and the gospel. When something is really good it is a shame to spoil it by not correcting our small faults. Little things can ruin our influence for good. Watch out for little flies! *—TNSDB*

Therefore encourage one another and build one another up, just as you are doing. —1 Thessalonians 5:11

Are we encouraging one another? Working to encourage and guide one another in the Christian faith is much too rare these days. —*TNSDB*

I have known many ministers who wanted to know how they could keep their congregation out of the world. Give them so much to do that they won't have time to indulge worldly influences.

—*D. L. Moody, Each with His Work*

[Our fathers] murmured…
    and did not obey the voice of the LORD.
They angered [the LORD] at the waters of Meribah,
    and it went ill with Moses on their account,
for they made his spirit bitter,
    and he spoke rashly with his lips. —Psalm 106:25, 32-33

Moses was the meekest man on the earth (Numbers 12:3) and even he spoke in anger. We have no perfect example except the Lord Jesus. He was never provoked and never spoke unadvisedly. May we be of the same mind as he was. "The anger of man does not produce the righteousness that God requires" (James 1:20). May we be delivered from getting angry, no matter how much we may be annoyed or irritated. —*TNSDB*

For I am not ashamed of the gospel, for it is the power of God for salvation to everyone who believes. —Romans 1:16

You have no reason to despair. If the ministers of Christ will only come back to preaching the gospel of Jesus Christ, plainly, simply, and with the Holy Spirit sent down from heaven, we will drive those who would replace the gospel with rituals or entertainment back to where they came, as our fathers did before us. Never lose your faith in the gospel. Always believe that our power is gone when we get away from the cross. But also believe this: When we come back to the truth as it is in Jesus, God glorifies his name. —Sermon #909 *Voices From the Excellent Glory*

re·mem·branc·er (noun) — a person with the job or responsibility of reminding others of something

Jesus is the Remembrancer of the promises; he reminds the Father about the promises he has made. He pleads with God to favor us, and points out the divine promise in our defense. "He…makes intercession for the transgressors." We may ask the Lord for the good things he has promised us, that he may do them for us; and these requests may be made under the most encouraging of circumstances, because the Lord Jesus himself becomes the Intercessor for us. For the church's sake he does not hold back, but day and night he is before the throne of grace reminding the Father of the blood with which he sealed and validated the promise. —*According to Promise*

Blessed are those who are persecuted for righteousness' sake, for theirs is the kingdom of heaven.

Blessed are you when others revile you and persecute you and utter all kinds of evil against you falsely on my account. Rejoice and be glad, for your reward is great in heaven, for so they persecuted the prophets who were before you.

—Matthew 5:10-12

The world cannot appreciate the character traits in which the Lord delights. That is why it opposes and hates them. As good soldiers of Jesus, our job is to endure the world's disapproval. Never flinch, even for a moment, at taking up your cross for Jesus' sake. —*TNSDB*

Let what you say be simply 'Yes' or 'No'; anything more than this comes from evil. —Matthew 5:37

Does this not forbid every kind of oath, not only profane swearing, but even that which is normally required by civil governments? Christians should avoid all expressions like "on my honor," "on my word." That kind of language goes beyond the "yes and no" that Christians should use. Men who swear profanely are only fooling themselves when they imagine that their oaths give them more credibility. Every sensible person knows that a man who is usually swearing profanely is quite able both to lie and to steal. Clean language becomes those who have been washed in the blood of Jesus. The tongue is an indicator of the health of both soul and body. He who is not pure in word is certainly not pure in heart and will not see the Lord. —*TNSDB*

Love your enemies and pray for those who persecute you, so that you may be sons of your Father who is in heaven. For he makes his sun rise on the evil and on the good, and sends rain on the just and on the unjust. —Matthew 5:44-45

Our only weapon against evil is good. Never stop using it, cost us what it may. The love of God falls on men who do not deserve it and so also must our kindness. It would be far better if a hundred evil people received our help by deceiving us than that one suffering fellow creature should be neglected because of the wickedness of others. Hardness of heart gradually grows on men through contact with a deceitful and harsh world, but we must not allow evil influences to control us and harden our hearts against our fellows. —*TNSDB*

True religion will always suffer
when men try to defend it with force.

You therefore must be perfect, as your heavenly Father is perfect. —Matthew 5:48

This is a high ideal, but we must aim to reach it. Kindness to all and love that cannot be conquered are the crown and glory of a holy character. Without them we still come up short, no matter what other virtues we may have. The man of uncompromising fairness must rise even higher and become the meek man who forgives injuries and is the generous friend of the needy. Oh God of love, instruct us to this level, for Jesus' sake. —*TNSDB*

"He will quiet you by his love" —Zephaniah 3:17

My heart is comforted when I read these words of unchanging, enduring, eternal love. Jehovah does not change. He is married to his people and he hates divorce. Immutability is written on his heart; he is unable to change. Doves mate for life; they remain faithful until death; and if one dies, the other, in many cases, will languish away in grief, because both lives were wrapped up in each other. In much the same way our Lord has chosen his beloved and he will never change. He died for his church, and as long as he lives he will remember his own precious church, and what it cost him. "Who shall separate us from the love of Christ?" "He will quiet you by his love."

—Sermon #1990 *A Sermon for the Present Time*

God forbid that even one thought of pride should poison our spirit.

Beloved, I pray that all may go well with you and that you may be in good health, as it goes well with your soul.

—3 John 2

This is not a blessing many would be comfortable with. If their bodies thrived only as their souls do, many would die, and most professors of Christianity would be weak, poor, sick, and pathetic.

—*TNSDB*

JESUS—THE HEAVENLY ARK OF THE COVENANT

Certain brothers who have been accustomed to that style of praying known as Liturgy criticize us for our familiarity in prayer. They think we are too bold and arrogant in drawing so near to God. Brothers, we are not amazed at your judgment, nor will we complain about it. We would not condemn you for your distant prayers, but we cannot give in to your disapproval of our bolder approach. We have a sense of acceptance in our hearts and "the Spirit of adoption" will not let us talk about God in any other way than as favored children. We come to the throne of grace boldly because we come through Jesus. Who is afraid of Jesus? Who trembles when drawing near to him? And if he is the mercy seat to which we come, and that is the place where the Father meets us, then we feel that he allows this holy familiarity, and the humble freedom that the Spirit of adoption suggests to our hearts.

— Sermon #1621 *The Ark of the Covenant*

THE SINLESS ONE

A clear proof that the Bible comes from God is supplied by its description of the perfect man. Jesus is sinless in thought, and word and deed. His enemies cannot find a fault in him of either excess or defect. We do not find another portrait of a perfect man anywhere else in the world. Jesus is unique. He is original, with characteristics all his own, but without any straying from the straight line of righteousness. He lived in the fierce light of a king among men, interacting with the world in a thousand ways. He instilled a way of life that far excelled any other, and practiced what he taught. Above all, he crowned the living of a perfect life with the surrender of himself to death for his enemies. From where did this portrait come if the man never existed? No painter goes beyond his own ideal; no imperfect mind could have invented the perfect mind of Christ. The record is divine. —*The Clue of the Maze*

This is the blood of the covenant that God commanded for you. —Hebrews 9:20

Under the law, blood was seen everywhere. It was essential to its teachings. The blood of Jesus is the very life of the gospel. A ministry without the blood of Jesus in it is dead and worthless.

"Indeed, under the law almost everything is purified with blood, and without the shedding of blood there is no forgiveness of sins" (Hebrews 9:22). This all-important truth needs to be learned well and remembered. Nothing can cleanse us except the blood of Jesus. Sacraments, prayers, regrets are all useless as a substitute for faith in the blood. Let us rest on the "once for all" offered atonement, and, in humble faith, know that we are fully accepted. —*TNSDB*

I never saw anyone living for this world that was satisfied; but Christ satisfies the longings of the heart.
—*D. L. Moody, Christ's Call to Peter*

The one who waters will himself be watered. —Proverbs 11:25

Every one of us should think about how we can be a blessing to others. Those of you who are going around with your hearts sad and cast down, if you go to work and try to help others, then your burdens will be gone and the light will shine in your souls.

—D. L. Moody *Message to Christian Workers*

SALVATION IS ALL A GIFT

This is the gospel that we are sent to preach to you: "God so loved the world, that he gave his only Son, that whoever believes in him should not perish but have eternal life" (John 3:16). "This is the testimony, that God gave us eternal life, and this life is in his Son" (1 John 5:11). On God's part it is all giving; on our part it is all receiving. The promise is already made, and it is made freely; it will be fulfilled, and it will be fulfilled freely.

God does not begin with giving, and then go on to charging a price. No commission is payable upon receipt of his grace. He does not ask or receive a penny; his love is completely a gift. You may accept his promise as a gift; he will not lower himself by listening to any other terms. —*According to Promise*

MAY 30

My God will supply every need of yours according to his riches in glory in Christ Jesus. —Philippians 4:19

This is a grand assurance. God is the giver; his infinite glory is the storehouse. Jesus guarantees the delivery and the supply is unlimited. What more can anyone ask for? The promissory note from the Bank of Faith makes all believers rich beyond a miser's dream. —*TNSDB*

THE PROMISE OF SALVATION IS A GIFT

They say, "There is nothing freer than a gift." Why should my reader not receive this gift as well as myself? To the one who is willing to give, a person's poverty is more a recommendation than an obstacle. So then, come, you who have no merit, Christ will be your merit. Come, you who have no righteousness, he will be your righteousness. Come, you who are filled to the brim with sin, the pardoning Lord will put away your sin. Come, you who are completely miserable, and be made rich in Jesus.

The business of begging suits you, and you will prosper in it, because I see you have a cruel hunger, and an empty wallet. The person who cannot work should not be ashamed to beg. A beggar needs no goods to sell. Worn-out shoes and worn-out clothes make a proper uniform for a beggar. Are you dressed this way spiritually? The poorer the person, the more welcome they are at the door of divine charity. The less you have of your own, the more welcome you are to "ask God, who gives generously to all without reproach." —*According to Promise*

JUNE 1

THE PHARISEES AND THE MAN BLIND FROM BIRTH

They answered him, "You were born in utter sin, and would you teach us?" And they cast him out. —John 9:34

Fault finding and persecution are the old weapons of those who have all of their arguments answered, but refuse to be convinced. We must expect such things in the same proportion as our enemies feel the power of our words.

He was convinced the man who gave him his sight was at least a prophet and he was not ashamed to proclaim it. When he knew more, he was just as definite and outspoken. If the Lord has given us spiritual sight, we should be just as ready to be as positive and outspoken as this remarkable man. The cause of God needs many champions right now who will speak out for Jesus whether it offends or pleases those who hear. May the Lord make us like this man. —*TNSDB*

JUNE 2

Do not judge by appearances, but judge with right judgment. —John 7:24

Excellent advice! We would all do well to follow it. We should not allow ourselves to be swayed by the prejudice of others or influenced by first impressions. Good men and good things are often despised. Truth and holiness have often been criticized and abused by mankind. All is not gold that glitters and there is much real gold that never glitters at all. May we be taught by the Holy Spirit to hate that which is evil and admire that which is good and true. May we always be found on the Savior's side. —*TNSDB*

I acknowledged my sin to you, and I did not cover my iniquity. —Psalm 32:5

Godly people are sincere in acknowledging their sin. Hypocrites cover and smother their sin; they do not acknowledge their sin but conceal it. They are like a patient with some horrible disease, that would rather die than acknowledge they are sick; but the sincerity of godly people is seen in this—they will confess and be ashamed of their sin. "Behold, I have sinned, and I have done wickedly" (2 Samuel 24:17). No, a child of God will be specific about confessing sin. Weak Christians will confess sin wholesale; they will acknowledge sin in general, but they will not, as David did, point to the particular fault: "For I know my transgressions" (Psalm 51:3). He does not say, I have done evil, but points to his specific sin.

—Thomas Watson (1620-1686)

Be glad. —Psalm 32:11

Happiness is not only our privilege, but our duty. We really do serve a generous God; he makes our being joyful part of our obedience. How sinful is our rebellious complaining! It seems only natural that a person blessed with forgiveness should be glad! We read about someone who died at the foot of the scaffold from the great joy he had after receiving a pardon from his king; and shall we receive the free pardon from the King of kings and yet wallow in inexcusable sorrow? —*The Treasury of David*

JUNE 5

We hear that some among you walk in idleness, not busy at work, but busybodies. Now such persons we command and encourage in the Lord Jesus Christ to do their work quietly and to earn their own living. —2 Thessalonians 3:11-12

Some eat other people's food almost their whole lives. It is pleasant to help the needy, but it is a hard task to have to support the lazy. Young people should strive to ease their parents as soon as possible from the job of supporting them. And those who receive help from the church should make it a matter of conscience to never take a penny more than they absolutely need. —*TNSDB*

JUNE 6

PHILIP AND THE ETHIOPIAN EUNUCH READING FROM ISAIAH

It was the finger of God that pointed to this passage; because the grand total of all Christian truth is Christ, both humbled and exalted. This passage contains authoritative advice for all teachers: The most important thing is leading souls to the knowledge of Christ, the Crucified and the Risen One. As a rule, this is much more effective than preaching right and wrong. The missionaries to Greenland who, with sermons on the living God and his holy commandments, preached for a whole year to deaf ears, struck home when they changed to the evangelical message, "Behold, the Lamb of God, who takes away the sin of the world!"

—*Lange's Commentary* (circa 1852)

And the LORD turned to [Gideon] and said, "Go in this might of yours and save Israel from the hand of Midian; do not I send you?" "I will be with you." —Judges 6:14,16

How inspired must Gideon have been when "the Lord turned to him" and spoke to him. God told Gideon to "go in this might of yours" and made him mighty. He sent him on his mission and went with him. He taught him faith and then honored his faith. How will the Lord glorify himself in each of us? —*TNSDB*

That night the LORD said to [Gideon]..., "Build an altar to the LORD your God." —Judges 6:25-26

Gideon is told to start right away and get rid of everything in his house that is used to worship the false god. Those who want to serve God in a foreign country should begin by serving God at home. He was not commanded to dedicate Baal's temple to God, but to destroy it. He was not ordered to sacrifice to God on the idol's altar, but to destroy it. We cannot overdo it when it comes to cleaning out the things that tempt us. The filthy birds of sin will return if we do not destroy their dirty nests. God gave Gideon a wonderful job to do. We should rejoice if he gives us a special assignment. —*TNSDB*

WHEN GIDEON TESTED THE LORD WITH THE FLEECE
—Judges 6:36-40

See how tenderly the Lord looks on the weakness of his servant's faith and gives a double miracle to strengthen his confidence. The Lord also gives assurance of his presence to strengthen our faith. Sometimes during the Communion Service he will give us a special awareness of his grace, even though others do not experience it. On another occasion others rejoice in the abundance of the Lord's grace and we do not. If our religion was a lifeless machine, we could adjust it to always act the same way. If it were merely rituals and ceremonies, we could always keep it from changing. But because it is from the Lord, he is the one who decides when and where his almighty power will be made evident.

—TNSDB

JUNE 10

THE SHIPWRECK WHEN PAUL WAS
TAKEN TO ROME AS A PRISONER

The soldiers' plan was to kill the prisoners, lest any should swim away and escape. —Acts 27:42

The soldiers were responsible for the prisoners. The penalty for allowing them to escape was death. Therefore we should not be surprised by their cruel plan of action.

But the centurion, wishing to save Paul, kept them from carrying out their plan. He ordered those who could swim to jump overboard first and make for the land, and the rest on planks or on pieces of the ship. And so it was that all were brought safely to land. —Acts 27:43-44

We see here the promise of God kept to the letter. The danger was great, but everyone was saved from death. God has never broken his word and he never will. It is only right that we should believe his promises without thinking twice. If we do trust his promises, then our lives will be free from care, and we will have good reasons to rejoice every day. May unbelief be thrown overboard this day and childlike confidence rule our lives.

—TNSDB

Then the king promoted Shadrach, Meshach, and Abednego in the province of Babylon. —Daniel 3:30

The unwavering loyalty of these three holy young men is an example we should follow. They never hesitated or tried to discuss options with the tyrant. Their hearts were anchored in God. They were confident that they had made the right decision. As a result, they conquered the proud king, triumphed over death itself, and overcame the brute force of the flames. Their reward was greater than immense wealth. Jesus walked in the intense flames with them and turned the fiery furnace into a grand palace. Let us hold tightly to the truth that is in Jesus without flinching and no evil will come near us. When it comes to God and his holy gospel, let us never debate or question. Rather, let us be bold to sacrifice even life itself if it becomes necessary. May the sons of this family be such young men as Shadrach, Meshach, and Abednego. Amen.

—TNSDB

Ask, and It Will Be Given. —Matthew 7:7

To the one who is willing to give, a person's poverty is more a recommendation than an obstacle. So then, come, you who have no merit, Christ will be your merit. Come, you who have no righteousness, he will be your righteousness. Come, you who are filled to the brim with sin, the pardoning Lord will put away your sin. Come, you who are completely miserable, and be made rich in Jesus. *—According to Promise*

Do not be afraid; you have done all this evil. Yet do not turn aside from following the LORD. —1 Samuel 12:19-25

The natural tendency of this kind of [ungodly] fear is to turn aside from following the Lord. "But do not be afraid," said Samuel. "Turn away from that fear that turns you away from God." Their sin caused their fear, just as it caused Adam and their fathers to be afraid. It was a fear that turned them aside to empty things that cannot profit or deliver. He told them they had sinned, yet not to fear with that fear that would make them turn aside. Sinner, do you see this? When the greatness of your sins has such a hold on you that your fear of God causes you to run away from him in your heart, your fear of God is ungodly. It is more wicked and ungodly than the sins that caused your fear. Samuel rebuked this fear and told them of another fear, the true fear of God. "Fear the LORD," he said, "and serve him faithfully with all your heart." Furthermore he encouraged them to do so by saying, "For the LORD will not forsake his people" (1 Samuel 12:24).

—John Bunyan, *The Fear of God*

Isaac went out to meditate in the field toward evening.

—Genesis 24:63

This good man chose a quiet and private place for one of the most heavenly of occupations. He is an example to every one of us. If we meditated more we would be far more gracious than we are. —*TNSDB*

Our Redeemer from of old is your name. —*from* Isaiah 63

Dr. Robert Hawker (1753-1827) has the following spiritual thoughts on this very wonderful chapter:

"Who is this that comes up with salvation, but the LORD mighty to save? He is one with Jehovah in the divine nature and no less one with us in the human nature. He is bone of our bone and flesh of our flesh. Surely, LORD, your own arm brought salvation and of the people there was no one with you. In all things you were required to be made like your brethren, but in your redemption-work, you walked in the winepress of the wrath of God alone. In the midst of all our rebellions and forgetfulness of you, you never forgot us or ignored our interest. In all our afflictions you were afflicted. Your love and your pity never decreased, because you were always Jesus; 'the same yesterday and today and forever.' Oh! then, Lord! do not let the waywardness of your children stand in the way of the gracious designs of your love. Remember that we are only dust and let 'your zeal and your might' and 'the stirring of your inner parts and your compassion' never be held back. We throw ourselves on your covenant relationship with us and plead of you, our God, to remember that most blessed promise, in which you said, 'I will not turn away from doing good' and, 'I will put the fear of me in their hearts, that they may not turn from me'" (Jeremiah 32:40). —*TNSDB*

I am he who comforts you; who are you that you are afraid of man who dies...Where is the wrath of the oppressor?
—Isaiah 51:12-13

It is in God's hands. No oppressor can rage against us unless the Lord allows it. Then why are we afraid? He who gives our enemy permission to annoy us to a point, holds the other end of his chain and will keep him within bounds. In holy confidence let us stand still and see the salvation of God. —*TNSDB*

The enemy took all the possessions of Sodom and Gomorrah…. They also took Lot…who was dwelling in Sodom, and his possessions, and went their way

—Genesis 14:11-12

"All is not gold that glitters." Moving to Sodom turned out to be a poor choice for Lot. Believers who try to follow the ways of the world should not be surprised when they suffer for doing so. Lot went to Sodom in the hope of gaining wealth. Now he loses everything in one blow. If we put too much effort into growing rich, the Lord can take everything away in a moment in time.

—*TNSDB*

A gracious heart will never rejoice in the misfortune of others, no matter how cruel they may have been.

For my father and my mother have forsaken me, but the LORD will take me in. —Psalm 27:10

Our dear parents will be the last to desert us. But even if the milk of human kindness should dry up, there is a heavenly Father who will never forget us. Some of the greatest saints in history have been kicked out of their families and "persecuted for righteousness' sake" (Matthew 5:10). —*TNSDB*

FAITH MUST BE FOR EVERY DAY

God is one. God's works and his ways are one. His laws for earth are found in the same book of laws as those for heaven. The natural world and the spiritual world are not in conflict. The line between religious and non-religious is imaginary and harmful. We believe God for time as well as for eternity, for earth as well as for heaven, for the body as well as for the soul. An honest person must not confine faith in God to certain mysterious and intangible concerns. There should be no doubting God when it comes to immediate concerns and the trials of everyday life. We are taught by our great Master to pray to the heavenly Father, "Your kingdom come," and the same prayer includes the request, "Give us this day our daily bread." To tell heaven about our greater cares, and leave the smaller ones to unbelief, would be as unwise as to post a guard at the door of the house, but expressly command him to pay no attention to an open window. —*The Clue of the Maze*

Therefore, since we have been justified by faith, we have peace with God through our Lord Jesus Christ. —Romans 5:1

There are people who are at peace with God concerning the forgiveness of sin, and they agree with his will to a point; but they are not walking carefully in the path of obedience, and so they are missing the sense of divine love. God is their Father, and he loves them, but he hides his face from them. They walk in a way that opposes his will, and so he walks in a way that opposes them. Such a situation will not bring the fullest peace.

—Sermon #1343 *The Jewel of Peace*

JUNE 21

I am the light of the world. Whoever follows me will not walk in darkness, but will have the light of life. —John 8:12

I have seen a picture recently that I don't enjoy a great deal. It represents Christ knocking at the door with a lantern. What need does the Son of God have for a lantern? Christ says, "I am the light of the world;" he doesn't need any lantern. Did you ever find a man or woman anywhere in Christendom that was following the Son of God that was in darkness?... A person who is following Christ can't help but be in light, because Christ is the light of the world. Yes, and that light carries us beyond the grave and beyond the judgment. We don't fear death. It can't be very dark, because Christ is there. —D. L. Moody *God is Love*

Victory over this wicked world involves struggle.

JUNE 22

And I am sure of this, that he who began a good work in you will bring it to completion at the day of Jesus Christ.
—Philippians 1:6

This delightful confidence is the crowning joy of the Christian life. If he who began the good work did not also carry it on we would be in a miserable predicament. But, blessed be God, the work of grace is in the hands of one who never leaves his work unfinished. —*TNSDB*

[When the Son of Man comes in his glory he] will say to those on his right, "Come, you who are blessed by my Father, inherit the kingdom prepared for you from the foundation of the world. For I was hungry and you gave me food, I was thirsty and you gave me drink, I was a stranger and you welcomed me, I was naked and you clothed me, I was sick and you visited me, I was in prison and you came to me."

—Matthew 25:34-36

These are all acts of love; not one of them consists of words or official rituals. The truest worship of God is charity to the needy. Does not the apostle James tell us, "Religion that is pure and undefiled before God, the Father, is this: to visit orphans and widows in their affliction, and to keep oneself unstained from the world" (James 1:27). *—TNSDB*

Then the righteous will answer him, saying, "Lord, when did we see you hungry and feed you, or thirsty and give you drink? And when did we see you a stranger and welcome you, or naked and clothe you? And when did we see you sick or in prison and visit you?" And the King will answer them, "Truly, I say to you, as you did it to one of the least of these my brothers, you did it to me." —Matthew 25:37-39

They did these acts of love without trying to draw attention to themselves. They did not consider them important enough for others to congratulate them over. But the Judge of heaven and earth saw them as excellent and will declare them publicly before men and angels. They had only been kind to poor and afflicted men and women and were surprised to hear the Lord regarded their actions as done to him. The Lord honors true charity! "Whoever is generous to the poor lends to the LORD" (Proverbs 19:17). Who would not show kindness to his Redeemer? *—TNSDB*

You surround me with shouts of deliverance. —Psalm 32:7

This word "surround" implies that as we are overwhelmed on every side with troubles, so we are surrounded with just as many comforts and deliverances. As our crosses grow daily, so our comforts increase day by day. We are attacked on every side and on every side defended. Therefore, we should express our praise for God on every side, as David says, "Bless the LORD, O my soul, and all that is within me" (Psalm 103:1).

—Archibald Symson (1564-1628).

Do not disbelieve, but believe. —John 20:27

Dear Friends, if you began to seek signs, and if you were to see them, do you know what would happen? Why, you would want more; and when you had these, you would demand still more. Those who live by their feelings judge the truth of God by their own emotions. When they feel happy, then they believe; but if their spirits sink, if the weather happens to be a little damp, or if they are not well, down go their spirits, and, right away, down goes their faith. The person who lives by a faith that does not depend on feelings, but is built on the Word of the Lord, will remain as steady and firm as the mountain of God. But the one who craves for this thing and that thing, as a sign that the Lord's hand is guiding them, is in danger of perishing from lack of faith. No one will perish, if they have even a grain of living faith, because God will deliver them from the temptation; but the temptation is very trying to one's faith. —Sermon #2061 *The Cure for Doubts*

Keep me as the apple of your eye. —Psalm 17:8

No part of the body is more precious, more tender, and more carefully guarded than the eye. And no part of the eye is more especially protected than the central apple, or the pupil. The Hebrew calls it, "the daughter of the eye." The All-wise Creator has placed the eye in a well protected position. It is surrounded by protruding bones, like Jerusalem is encircled by mountains. Its great Creator has also surrounded it with many layers of inward covering: The hedge of the eyebrows, the curtain of the eyelids, and the fence of the eyelashes. In addition, God has made us value our eyes so much and protect them from danger so quickly that no part of the body is more cared for than the organ of sight. Lord, protect me because I trust I am one with Jesus and therefore a part of the spiritual body of Christ. —*TNSDB*

Jesus answered them, "Have faith in God. Truly, I say to you, whoever says to this mountain, 'Be taken up and thrown into the sea,' and does not doubt in his heart, but believes that what he says will come to pass, it will be done for him."

—Mark 11:22-23

When the Lord grants faith about anything, it is the shadow of the coming event. The prayer of faith is always heard, but faith is not given in all cases. We cannot always pray in full assurance and in such cases it would be sinful presumption to pretend to have unlimited power in prayer. Our prayers are limited to the will of God. Our guidelines to that limitation are the promises of God and the faith he gives us in the matter. —*TNSDB*

"Therefore I tell you, whatever you ask in prayer, believe that you have received it, and it will be yours." —Mark 11:24

This does, of course, take for granted that we pray for right things. Otherwise, we ask and do not receive, because we ask wrongly, to spend it on our passions (James 4:3). What freedom in prayer is given us here! How slow we are to use the power that we have been entrusted with! —*TNSDB*

God exceeds our desire; he never comes short in what concerns our spiritual and eternal good. —*Arthur Lake (1569-1626)*

The tongue is a fire, a world of unrighteousness. The tongue is set among our members, staining the whole body, setting on fire the entire course of life, and set on fire by hell. —James 3:6

The tongue is a singular part of our body. God has given man two ears, one to hear instructions of human knowledge, the other to listen to his divine teaching. Two eyes, one so he can see his way, another to pity and sympathize with his distressed brothers and sisters in Christ. Two hands, one with which to work for his own living, the other to relieve his brother's needs. Two feet, one to walk on ordinary days to his ordinary labor, the other to walk on sacred days in the company of the congregation of the saints. Yet he has given man only one tongue; that he may instruct him to hear twice as much as he speaks, and to walk and work twice as much as he talks. —Thomas Adams (1583-1653)

CARRY YOUR CHECKBOOK

It is good for Christians who encounter many trials to carry their checkbook in their pocket, but notice what kind of checkbook I mean. Get a copy of a Bible Promise Book—one with a good table of contents or subject index, with the promises of God conveniently arranged for easy use. I usually carry a copy in my pocket, so that when I have had some particular trouble, I can turn to the subject that deals with my problem, and I can always find a promise to meet the need. Or, whenever your trial comes, go home to your Bible, open it, ask the Lord to direct you, and with a little search I think you will soon find a promise that was made especially for you. It may have ideally suited twenty cases before you, but only you can say if an angel had come down from heaven to bring a message precisely fitted to your distinct trial, it could not have been worded better, the arrow could not have hit the center of the target more surely than it has.

—Sermon #440 *Cheer for the Fainthearted*

Behold, for your iniquities you were sold, and for your transgressions your mother was sent away. —Isaiah 50:1

When Israel was carried into captivity it was not because God had forgotten his covenant or cruelly thrown away his people. He was not like a cruel husband who divorces his wife in anger or like a poor needy father forced to give up his children to his creditors for debt. No, it was sin that brought every evil on Israel. Sin, and nothing else. This is also true in our case. Sin is the source of our misery. If we rebel against God, he will surely make us feel the sting of his displeasure. —*TNSDB*

Thus says the LORD, the God…"I will give them one heart and one way, that they may fear me forever, for their own good and the good of their children after them. I will make with them an everlasting covenant, that I will not turn away from doing good to them. And I will put the fear of me in their hearts, that they may not turn from me." —Jeremiah 32:39-40

These are words of love and belong as much to every child of God as to restored Israel. There is only one everlasting covenant and all believers have an interest in it. The people of God are favored with new natures that lead them toward God and holiness. This is the certain result of being born again and is a blessing that words cannot fully describe. If it were possible to fall away and perish even after conversion, we would have no assurance. But if the Lord declares "they may not turn from me," our final perseverance is certain. *—TNSDB*

GOD'S INVOLVEMENT IN OUR LIFE

God is not an inactive power far, far away. Trusting in him is not a dreamy fairytale dependence. It is asked whether God ever does work for the benefit of those who trust him; and it is hinted that he is too busy with other things, and will not stoop to the insignificant cares of men and women. This is obviously wrong. God is at work at our doors and in our homes; yes, in our bodies and in our minds. The child's father is very busy, but he is busy in the same room where his needy child is; and therefore he is right where he needs to be. *—The Clue of the Maze*

JULY 5

Why, O Lord, do you stand far away? Why do you hide yourself in times of trouble? — Psalm 10:1

The refiner is never far from the mouth of the furnace when his gold is in the fire, and the Son of God is always walking in the midst of the flames when his holy children are thrown into them.

—The Treasury of David

If we live for God, and have any spiritual light,
it is because Jesus Christ makes it happen.

JULY 6

His divine power has granted to us all things that pertain to life and godliness...by which he has granted to us his precious and very great promises, so that through them you may become partakers of the divine nature, having escaped from the corruption that is in the world because of sinful desire.

—2 Peter 1:3-4

Jesus taught us to say, "Give us this day our daily bread." Therefore, we are neither ashamed nor afraid to ask all things from him. We live a life of dependence and should delight in that fact. It is sweet to take all things from the hands of our crucified Lord. Happy is the poverty that leads us to be rich in Christ. We earn nothing and yet receive everything. We are blessed in being hourly receivers of the gift of God. "He has granted to us his precious and very great promises." *—According to Promise*

And Samuel prayed to the LORD. —1 Samuel 8:6

This little sentence is most instructive. When we are perplexed or displeased, we should turn immediately to prayer. We continually read of the prayers of the Lord Jesus. We ought to imitate him in this. As the fish loves the stream, and the bird the branch, so the believer loves prayer. —*TNSDB*

WHEN SAMUEL WAS ABOUT TO
ANOINT SAUL KING OVER ISRAEL.

As they were going down to the outskirts of the city, Samuel said to Saul, "Tell the servant to pass on before us, and when he has passed on, stop here yourself for a while, that I may make known to you the word of God.

—1 Samuel 9:27

Today, let each of us do our best to have a little time for thought and prayer; while we keep these words in our hearts, "Stop here yourself for a while, that I may make known to you the word of God." —*TNSDB*

When all the elders of Israel gathered together and came to Samuel and said to him, "Behold, now appoint for us a king to judge us like all the nations," Samuel said to them:

"But today you have rejected your God, who saves you from all your calamities and your distresses, and you have said to him, 'Set a king over us.'" —1 Samuel 10:19

The Lord's people often refuse to walk by faith. This is just one example of an evil that is all too common among them. They are not spiritual enough to trust only in the invisible God. They want to depend on something they can see. They are not satisfied with the unseen hand of God helping them. They demand visible assistance. They cry out for help the same way the world does. The Lord often gives these people just what they ask for. However, it soon becomes more of a curse than a blessing—just as it was for Saul and Israel. When we pray we should always say, "Not as I will, but as you will" (Matthew 26:39). If we pray thinking we know more about what is good for us than God does, he may answer our prayer in anger and the result will not be one that brings real happiness. —*TNSDB*

JULY 10

WHEN SAUL WAS APPOINTED KING OVER ISRAEL

But some worthless fellows said, "How can this man save us?" —1 Samuel 10:27a

No one can hope to please everybody. Even the man God himself selects is not approved by people who are never satisfied. Saul was from a good family, he had good character, he was humble, and he was pleasant. But these things did not count for anything with these troublemakers. May none of us ever belong to that evil class of persons, who are always in opposition, always faultfinding, and never willing to work with anybody. This is not the mind of Christ, nor is it the fruit of the Spirit, which is always peaceable.

And they despised him and brought him no present. But he held his peace. —1 Samuel 10:27b

This was a very sensible thing to do. The man who can be quiet will defeat his enemies. Do not be quick to defend yourself, or answer those who lie about you. "Fear not, stand firm, and see the salvation of the Lord" (Exodus 14:13). —*TNSDB*

JULY 11

To those who are elect...according to the foreknowledge of God the Father. —1 Peter 1:1-2

Everyone who calls on the name of the Lord will be saved.

—Romans 10:13

Now, the elect must be saved, because there is no hellfire reserved for them. God has predestinated them to eternal life, and they will never perish, and no one will snatch them out of Christ's hand. God does not choose someone and then throw him or her away. He does not elect them and then throw them into the pit of hell. Now, you are elect. You could not have called if you had not been elected. Your election is the reason why you called. In view of the fact that you have called, and do call on the name of God, you are God's elect. —Sermon #140 *A Simple Sermon for Seeking Souls*

JULY 12

Be watchful. Your adversary the devil prowls around like a roaring lion, seeking someone to devour. Resist him, firm in your faith, knowing that the same kinds of suffering are being experienced by your brotherhood throughout the world.

—1 Peter 5:8-9

If we were the only ones who were tempted by the devil we might be terrified. But since he is the common enemy of all believers, and since each in their turn has defeated him, let us be bold in facing the devil. Let it be said of us as it was of Christian in *Pilgrim's Progress,*

> "The man so bravely played the man
> He made the fiend to fly." *—TNSDB*

Give, and it will be given to you. Good measure, pressed down, shaken together, running over, will be put into your lap.
—Luke 6:38

What makes the Dead Sea dead? Because it is all the time receiving, never giving out anything. Why is it that many Christians are cold? Because they are all the time receiving, never giving out anything. You go every Sunday and hear good sermons, and think that is enough. You are all the time receiving these grand truths, but never give them out. When you hear it, go and scatter the sacred truth abroad. Instead of having one minister to preach to a thousand people, this thousand ought to take a sermon and spread it until it reaches those that never go to church or chapel. Instead of having a few, we ought to have thousands using the precious talents that God has given them.

—D. L. Moody, *Each with His Work*

FAITH GUARDS THE DOOR

What is little? What is unimportant? To the wise person who wants to always do right there is no such thing. No, we must have a faith that is concerned about today, about our home, our job, our next meal. If our faith is only available on great occasions, we may be completely bewildered by the troubles for which our faith has no practical use. "The righteous shall live by his faith" (Habakkuk 2:4). Faith is not an outfit to wear only for going to church meetings; it is clothing for every day. Faith is all inclusive, universal, and constantly in operation. It is a principle that is always required by those who are in frequent danger and constantly in need. As the cherubim in the garden of Eden had "a flaming sword that turned every way to guard the way to the tree of life," so faith guards the soul from the advance of enemies, let them come from whatever direction they may. —*The Clue of the Maze*

JULY 15

She said to them, "Do not call me Naomi (pleasant or sweet)**; call me Mara** (or bitter)**, for the Almighty has dealt very bitterly with me. I went away full, and the LORD has brought me back empty.** —Ruth 1:20-21

God can soon change our sweets into bitters, therefore let us be humble. But he can just as easily transform our bitters into sweets. Therefore let us be hopeful. It is very usual for Naomi and Mara, sweet and bitter, to meet in the same person. He who was called Benjamin, or "the son of his father's right hand," was first called Benoni, or "the son of sorrow" (Genesis 35:18). The comforts of God's grace are all the sweeter when they follow the troubles of life.

When she had her husband, and sons, and property, she was full, and went her way to a foreign land, perhaps wrongly. But now that she was deprived of everything, she felt that God was with her in her emptiness, and that he had brought her back.

It is wise to know and appreciate that everything that happens to us is part of God's will for us. Naomi submitted to her Master even though she suffered from what seemed like harsh treatment. This is the proper kind of attitude for a believer to have who has been disciplined by God. Our Lord is the great example of it, for he said, "Shall I not drink the cup that the Father has given me?"

—TNSDB

JULY 16

So [Ruth] gleaned in the field until evening. Then she beat out what she had gleaned. —Ruth 2:17

The main reason Boaz was so kind to Ruth was that she was a guest in Israel, a dove nestling beneath Jehovah's wings. His religion was most important to him, and therefore he rejoiced that this woman had left everything to follow the living God. Meanwhile Ruth acted in the most modest and humble way. She was simply being herself. She was glad to work all day in the field to help support Naomi and herself. She considered it a pleasure to work for the benefit of someone who loved her so much. When children are kind to their parents, they are on the road to blessings. Little did Ruth imagine that she would one day be married to the owner of the fields in which she gleaned. There are good things in store for those who live correctly before God. —*TNSDB*

JULY 17

So Boaz took Ruth, and she became his wife…and she bore a son —Ruth 4:13

Here we see her self-denying faith rewarded. Ruth left behind her relatives, her country, and her hope for the future, to be with Naomi and the Lord's people. And the Lord not only blessed her, but blessed generations far into the future through her. Those who follow the Lord no matter what, will not be losers in the long run. To increase Ruth's joy and crown her happiness, the Lord gave her a son who was also a joy to Naomi. Here we find the reason the book of Ruth is included in the Bible. Ruth was the great-grandmother of King David, whose family line leads all the way to the birth of the Lord Jesus. All the Scriptures are intended to lead us in faith to the great Redeemer. May God grant that this purpose is or will be true in our case. —*TNSDB*

JULY 18

The LORD has remembered us; he will bless us; he will bless those who fear the LORD, both the small and the great.
—Psalm 115:12, 13

Past blessings guarantee the future, because our God does not change. These are precious promises for those who are very young, for those who live in poverty, for those who have little ability, and for those who are rejected by the world. They are not and will not be forgotten when God blesses his chosen. —*TNSDB*

JULY 19

Yet it was the will of the LORD to crush him; he has put him to grief. —Isaiah 53:10

Jehovah took pleasure in the atoning sacrifice. His love was so great that he crushed the Son of his love to save rebellious sinners. Yes, Jehovah himself put his own Son to grief. This is the way God proves his love for us. In return, we should give our entire lives to him. —*TNSDB*

"I am with you" is the very best encouragement in all the world.
(Haggai 2:4; Isaiah 41:10; Matthew 28:20)

JULY 20

He...was numbered with the transgressors; yet he bore the sin of many, and makes intercession for the transgressors.
—Isaiah 53:12

Those who genuinely trust in the Lord Jesus may rest assured that their sins have ceased to exist, because Jesus has paid their debt in full! They may also rejoice because the non-stop praying of our King and Intercessor keeps us safe. Let us come near to the cross of Jesus and rest our souls underneath the shadow of the Crucified One. God has provided himself a Lamb for a burnt offering. The victim is put to death, the promise is fulfilled, and believers are safe. Because of this, let us adore the Eternal Father from now to the end of eternity. —*TNSDB*

Would you not want us to rejoice at the sight and sense of the forgiveness of our sins?

Yes, but I would also have you trembling when God tells you that your sins are pardoned. I would have you, "Serve the LORD with fear, and rejoice with trembling" (Psalm 2:11). A joyful heart and wet eyes go together very well when you have a solid and godly joy. If God comes to you and visits you with the forgiveness of sins, and that visit removes the guilt, but increases the sense of your sinfulness, then that sense of God's presence will make you both rejoice and tremble. What a blessed embarrassment! You will stand before God as a wicked sinner and receive your pardon from his hand at the same time. You will receive the first fruits of your eternal salvation in such a way, "That you may remember and be confounded, and never open your mouth again because of your shame, when I atone for you for all that you have done, declares the Lord GOD" (Ezekiel 16:63). —John Bunyan, *The Fear of God*

THE CARES OF THE WORLD

When we experience pain we realize our bodies are real, and when we are weighed down by the cares of the world we feel the world is real. Yet the body is a poor tent and the world is a mere bubble. These visible things are not as substantial as they seem, but they appear solid to us. What we need to know is that the invisible is just as real as what we see, and even more so. We need a living God in this dying world. We must truly have him close to us or we will fail. The Lord is teaching his people to detect him; the promise is part of this educational process.

—*According to Promise*

May the LORD...send you help from the sanctuary!

—Psalm 20:2

When Jesus was praying at Gethsemane and facing death on the cross, an angel came from heaven and strengthened him (Luke 22:43). There is no other help like that which God sends and no other rescue like that which comes out of his sanctuary. For us, that sanctuary is the person of our blessed Lord who is pictured as the temple and the place of true protection that God has provided. Let us rush to the Cross for support anytime we have a need. Our God will send us help. The world despises our sanctuary help, but our hearts have learned to prize it more than any human aid. They look to human strength or money, but we turn to the sanctuary that is Jesus. —*TNSDB*

May the LORD...remember all your offerings! —Psalm 20:3

Before going to war, kings offered sacrifices. When their offering was accepted, it was a sign for success in the battle. Our blessed Lord presented himself as a sacrifice that was accepted by the Most High God as a pleasing aroma, after which he attacked and routed the fortified armies of hell. The sacrifice of Christ still perfumes the courts of heaven and continues to make the offerings and worship of his people acceptable. In our spiritual battles, we should never march forth to war until the Lord has given us a sign to proceed. Our faith should be in our bleeding Lord and his sacrifice for us. —*TNSDB*

Some trust in chariots and some in horses, but we trust in the name of the LORD our God. —Psalm 20:7

Chariots and horses were impressive and awe inspiring. Men took great pride in their modern weapons of war; their enemies were terrified by them. But the sharp eye of faith sees far more power in an invisible God than in even a huge army of chariots and horses. The most dreaded war machine in David's day was the war-chariot, armed with blades that mowed men down like grass. This is what the nations surrounding Israel gloried in and bragged about. But the saints considered the name of Jehovah to be a far better defense. The Lord did not allow the Israelites to keep warhorses, so it was only natural for them to have a great fear of the enemy's cavalry. We should admire the great faith of the bold singer who scorned even the great horses of Egypt when compared with the Lord of Hosts. Sadly, there are many in our time who profess to be the Lord's, but are hopelessly depending on other people and act as if they had never known the name of Jehovah at all! —*TNSDB*

While we were still sinners, Christ died for us. —Romans 5:8

If you just take your Bibles you will find that God loves you. There is no one in this wide world, sinner, that loves you like God loves you. You may think your father loves you, or your mother loves you, or a brother or a sister, but let me tell you, you can multiply it by ten thousand times ten thousand before it can equal God's love. "While we were still sinners, Christ died for us." Can you have greater proof of God's love and Christ's love? "Greater love has no one than this, that someone lay down his life for his friends." Christ laid down his life for his enemies. Ah, my friends, it will take all eternity for us to find out the height and breadth and length and depth of God's love. —D.L. Moody, *Christian Love*

LUKEWARMNESS

Oh, my brothers and sisters, have you ever really thought what an insult it is to God when we come before him with lukewarm prayers? There stands the Most Holy Place; the road to it is sprinkled with the precious blood of Jesus. Yet we come to it with cold hearts, or we approach it leaving our hearts behind. We kneel in the attitude of prayer, yet we do not pray. We chatter meaningless words, we express thoughts that are not our real desires, we pretend to have wants that we do not feel. Are we not showing disrespect for the Most Holy Place? We make it more into a coffee shop in which to relax and chat, rather than an awe inspiring place where we wrestle with God, and plead the blood of Christ while we sprinkle the place with the sweat and tears of our impassioned prayers. —Sermon #2802 *Lukewarmness*

Faith and common sense are closely related.

That by all means I might save some. —1 Corinthians 9:22b

True religion is to roll up the shirt sleeves and to fight the battle for Christ, and to go out among people as a humble worker, "That by all means I might save some." This is what your Lord wants you to do, this is the untying of the straps of his sandals.

—Sermon #1044 *Untying the Sandals*

The boastful shall not stand before your eyes; you hate all evildoers. —Psalm 5:5

What an astonishing thing is sin. It makes the God of love and Father of mercies an enemy to his creatures and can only be cleansed by the blood of the Son of God! All who believe the Bible must believe the sinfulness of sin; but they who have the deepest sense of it have only a weak understanding of its depth. It will never be fully comprehended in this world.

—Thomas Adam *(1701-1784) Private Thoughts on Religion*

Thomas Adam was an evangelical minister in the Church of England. He shepherded the same church for fifty-eight years, "Never wishing to change and repeatedly resisting pressure put upon him to look higher." *Private Thoughts on Religion* was published posthumously. The entry is from his private diary, "Which were meant for no eyes but his own."

Our beloved brother Paul also wrote to you according to the wisdom given him.... There are some things in them that are hard to understand, which the ignorant and unstable twist to their own destruction, as they do the other Scriptures.

—2 Peter 3:15-16

Correct doctrine can be twisted to serve bad purposes. This is not the fault of the doctrine, but of the foolish or wicked minds that misapply it. We must not neglect the study of those great truths that Paul talks about. The people who force them to mean something else are ignorant. We should not be on their side of the disagreement. If we are well acquainted with the deep things of God we will, by God's grace, be all the less likely to abuse them.

—*TNSDB*

Clothe yourselves, all of you, with humility toward one another, for "God opposes the proud but gives grace to the humble." —1 Peter 5:5

In those days slaves would tie on, or clothe themselves with, white aprons to distinguish themselves from freemen. The original word used here very likely refers to that practice. We are not to act like lords, but stand apron-ed with humility, ready to serve our fellow Christians in a gentle, submissive manner. —*TNSDB*

A hard, domineering spirit toward weaker brothers
in Christ always brings God's discipline.

August 1

I will be merciful toward their iniquities, and I will remember their sins no more. —Hebrews 8:12

The Holy Spirit, after he has come to me as the Spirit of adoption, can no longer come to me as a spirit of slavery. He put that fear in us in the beginning (Romans 8:15). Those first fears were given to produce the faith to believe and call God, "Father, Father." I am united to Christ. I no longer stand before his Father in my own sins or best efforts, but in Christ's glorious righteousness. He will not throw away a member of his body, of his own flesh and bones. The Holy Spirit will not bring a spirit of slavery and fear of damnation to him who stands complete before God in the righteousness of Christ. That would be a contradiction!

—John Bunyan, *The Fear of God*

August 2

WHEN YOU SIN after you have received the Spirit of adoption and now cry to God, "Father, Father," your transgression is considered that of a child, not a slave. All that happens to you for that offense is the discipline of a father. "For what son is there whom his father does not discipline?" It is worth pointing out that the Holy Spirit rebukes those who, under their discipline for sin, forget to call God their Father. "Have you forgotten," said Paul, "the exhortation that addresses you as sons? 'My son, do not regard lightly the discipline of the Lord, nor be weary when reproved by him.'" Also, recognize that God's disciplining of his children for their sin is a sign of grace and love, not of wrath and damnation. Therefore, there is no longer a reason for this fear, because "The Lord disciplines the one he loves, and chastises every son whom he receives" (Hebrews 12:5, 6, 7).

—John Bunyan, *The Fear of God*

Some men came and told Jehoshaphat, "A great multitude is coming against you." Then Jehoshaphat was afraid and set his face to seek the LORD. —2 Chronicles 20:2-3

He not only feared these invaders because of their huge numbers, but because the Lord sent him the prophet to declare that God's anger would be shown (2 Chronicles 19:2-3). However, his fears drove him to prayer. When this is the case, things are certain to get better. Great troubles can only be met by great prayer. Let us use this certain cure when we meet with trials. —*TNSDB*

Cast your burden on the LORD, and he will sustain you; he will never permit the righteous to be moved. —Psalm 55:22

Let us dwell a moment on this verse, "Your burden." Whatever burden your God lays on you, lay it "on the Lord." In his wisdom, he brought this burden on you. In your wisdom, you should give it right back to him. God will give you your share of suffering. Accept it with cheerful patience and then take it back to him with confident assurance. "He will sustain you." He who placed the burden on you will also give you the strength to endure it. Everything you need, and then some, will be provided for you to live through all your labors and trials. "As your days, so shall your strength be" (Deuteronomy 33:25). "He will never permit the righteous to be moved." He may seem to move away from us, like a tree bends away from the windy storm, but he will never be moved like the tree that is torn up by the roots. The person who stands with God stands firm. Many seek to destroy the saints, but God has not allowed them to perish and he never will. The godly stand like pillars, "steadfast, immovable," to the glory of the Great Designer. —*TNSDB*

AUGUST 5

Remember me, O LORD...that I may glory with your inheritance. —Psalm 106:4-5

My weak friend. You used to be as bold as a lion in your witness for Christ, but now you turn tail and run. How can you be bold with all those inconsistencies? There was a time when you were brave enough to be a martyr, but now what a coward you are. Who could be surprised at your change when they know that secret sin has damaged your profession and made you weak as a kitten? I urge you to pray this prayer: "That I may glory with your inheritance." You will never again be able to boast in the Lord until you are restored. You must return to the day you first cried out, "Father, I have sinned against heaven and before you. I am no longer worthy to be called your son." My brother, my sister, come back even now and receive another application of the blood of Christ. Look to Jesus again. —Sermon #1454 *A Poor Man's Prayer*

AUGUST 6

But the hair of [Samson's] head began to grow again after it had been shaved. —Judges 16:22

Our gracious God does not throw away his servants. His grace is like the receding tide of the ocean. Just like Samson's hair, it returns as strong as ever. It is one of the wonders of God that he will not stop loving someone even when that person proves they do not deserve to be loved. —*TNSDB*

AUGUST 7

THE LORD FOLLOWS A SYSTEM where his chosen are kept in constant communication with him. We are not allowed to forget our heavenly Father. We are often at the throne of grace, blessing God for promises fulfilled, and pleading promises on which we rely. We pay countless visits to the throne of grace, because there is a promise to plead, and a God waiting to be gracious. Should we not be grateful because God has arranged things this way? Rather than showering us with unpromised blessings, he increases the value of his benefits by making them the subjects of his promises and the objects of our faith. We should praise the Lord for creating this plan. —*According to Promise*

AUGUST 8

They repay me evil for good. —Psalm 35:12

For the good David did by killing Goliath, and destroying his tens of thousands of the Philistines, and thereby saving his king and country, Saul and his attendants envied him, and sought to kill him. Our Lord Jesus Christ also, for all the good he did to the Jews, by healing their bodies of diseases, and preaching the gospel to them for the benefit of their souls, was rewarded with false accusations and persecution, and finally the shameful death of the cross. The people of God are mistreated in much the same way, but this is an evil that will not go unpunished; "If anyone returns evil for good, evil will not depart from his house" (Proverbs 17:13).

—John Gill (1697-1771)

Then Samuel said to Saul…, Because you have rejected the word of the LORD, he has also rejected you from being king."

—1 Samuel 15:16, 23

Nothing can make up for disobeying God's will. We may pretend to be very zealous for God's glory, but intentionally disobeying his commands will condemn us. Being religious on the outside is not a substitute for holiness. Saul put to death those who practiced witchcraft, but as long as he would not obey the Lord, he was as guilty as the fake witches he had executed. Idolatry was an obvious sin against Jehovah, but stubbornly disobeying his law was just as much a form of evil rebellion. May the Holy Spirit cause us to be obedient down to the last detail. Nothing short of this will prove that we are the true servants of the Lord. —*TNSDB*

The LORD said to Samuel, "How long will you grieve over Saul, since I have rejected him from being king over Israel?

—1 Samuel 16:1

It was both natural and right for the prophet to mourn over Saul's sin, but he must not be upset because the Lord punished him. Instead, he must continue with the work God has for him. We should grieve for any who sin in such a way that God becomes angry against them. But we must not rebel because of his judgments on them. "Shall not the Judge of all the earth do what is just?" (Genesis 18:25). When the wicked are thrown into hell, the saints in heaven do not complain to God because they feel sorry for the convicted sinners. They respect and support the wisdom of the most Holy God and worship him with admiration and awe.

—*TNSDB*

AUGUST 11

Pilate then called together the chief priests and the rulers and the people, and said to them... "I will therefore punish and release him." —Luke 23:16

This was a compromise, but a very wicked one. If the prisoner was guilty, then he should not be released. If he was innocent he should not be punished. Attempts to compromise between right and wrong are always failures. Honest people should avoid making the effort. —*TNSDB*

Important steps should not be taken in a hurry.
We can do in an hour what we cannot undo in a lifetime.

AUGUST 12

They cried out, "Away with him, away with him, crucify him!" Pilate said to them, "Shall I crucify your King?" The chief priests answered, "We have no king but Caesar."
—John 19:15

Pilate was being sarcastic when he said, "Shall I crucify your King?" It was as clear as the noonday sun that Jesus was not a dangerous rival of Caesar. How could he be the earthly king of the Jews when it was the Jews who were demanding his execution?

Are any of us, like these Jews, rejecting the kingship of Jesus? If we reject him in our day-to-day lives, then it will be just as fatal as if we rejected him in words. Lord Jesus, you are our King. Reign over us and in us, so that we may one day reign with you.
—*TNSDB*

Looking to Jesus…who for the joy that was set before him endured the cross, despising the shame. —Hebrews 12:2

For it is for your sake that I have borne reproach that dishonor has covered my face. —Psalm 69:7

First, they piled insulting accusations on our Lord and then they hurried him away to be crucified. They dragged him through the cruel mockery of a trial that was not a trial. They smeared his face with their spit and covered it with bruises. The misery and shame of the crown of thorns marked the final humiliation of Jesus by the Roman soldiers. Ah, blessed Lord, it was our shame that you were forced to endure! Nothing deserves to be hated and despised more than sin. Oh Lord, when you were made sin for us, you were called on to endure abuse and scorn. Blessed be your name. It is over now, but we owe you more than any heart can imagine for your amazing act of love. —*TNSDB*

Since it was the day of Preparation, and so that the bodies would not remain on the cross on the Sabbath (for that Sabbath was a high day), the Jews asked Pilate that their legs might be broken and that they might be taken away.

—John 19:31

These men could commit this murder without shame. At the same time, however, they were great sticklers about keeping every one of their religious details. This proves that rites and ceremonies leave people as bad and cruel as they find them. The Roman church, with a thousand grand rituals, still rejoiced in the burning of godly men and women. They even invented The Rack and other ways to torture them. Let this teach us to give most of our attention to the spiritual requirements of the gospel, and remember that religion that does not change the heart and teach us to be merciful is good for nothing. —*TNSDB*

Then [Jesus] said to Thomas, "Put your finger here, and see my hands; and put out your hand, and place it in my side. Do not disbelieve, but believe." Thomas answered him, "My Lord and My God!" Jesus said to him, "Have you believed because you have seen me? Blessed are those who have not seen and yet have believed." —John 20:27-29

Our Redeemer's willingness to lower himself to our level is infinite. He understood the doubts Thomas had and, because he knew that Thomas was sincere and willing to be convinced, he agreed to his demands. A look was enough. The moment Thomas saw the wounds he understood that Jesus is Lord and God. This is a sweet lesson. May each of us learn to trust in Jesus again every day. The richest blessings are enjoyed by those who simply believe the word of God, even when they are surrounded with difficulties and have no visible sign that God will keep his word. The more childlike the faith the happier the heart. —*TNSDB*

For as by a man came death, by a man has come also the resurrection of the dead. For as in Adam all die, so also in Christ shall all be made alive. —1 Corinthians 15:21-22

The risen Savior is the promise and guarantee of our resurrection. We will certainly live again. Through Adam's sin all who belong to Adam die. And by Christ's righteousness all who belong to Christ will be made alive. There are two great covenant leaders. The first was Adam's leadership under the covenant of works, by which we have fallen. The second is the leadership of the Lord Jesus under the covenant of grace, by which we rise to eternal life. —*TNSDB*

You have one teacher. —Matthew 23:8

Ah, to learn who your true teacher is and serve only him as your master! We are willing to serve our friends, to serve the church, to serve the public, and please everyone, and forget the Lord. But we should have just one master, and live to please only him, and that person should be the Lord of glory. He is a good teacher and master. I want to recommend him to you. If he is not your master, then the devil is. Everyone has a master, and that master is either Satan or Christ. —D. L. Moody, *Six One Things*

Preaching that leads men away from the preacher himself and to his Lord is good preaching.

READER, WHAT IS YOUR RELATION WITH CHRIST?

Everything depends on your answer to this question. Are you depending on Christ alone? Then the Lord has promised to bless you, and do you good; and he will surprise you with the amazing ways in which he will do this for you. Nothing is too good for the Father to give to the person who delights in his Son Jesus.

—According to Promise

He was manifested in the flesh. — 1 Timothy 3:16

The truth about God manifest in flesh is great if you consider the great honor it gave to humanity. Mankind is greatly honored because God took the nature of man into union with himself. He did not take the nature of angels; he took on him the offspring and nature of Abraham! Of all God's creatures, whichever is closest to the Creator will obviously have the supremacy among all the ranks of creation. Which then will have reason to praise God the most? Shall the angels be chosen? Shall the swift winged sons of fire be first in heaven's royal court? Behold, and be astonished; a worm is preferred, a rebellious child of the earth is chosen! Human nature is married into oneness with the divine!

— Sermon #786 *The Great Mystery of Godliness*

Do not forsake me, O LORD!
   O my God, be not far from me!
Make haste to help me,
   O Lord, my salvation! —Psalm 38:21-22

God is not only our Savior, but our salvation. The person who has the Lord on their side already has salvation. In this last sentence, the eye of faith sees her prayers as being already answered and begins to glorify God for the mercy she expects to receive. Our heavenly Father will never forsake us. His grace will come to the rescue, and before long we will magnify his name for saving us out of all our troubles. Have we all repented of sin? Are we all resting by faith in him? —*TNSDB*

August 21

Like a sparrow in its flitting, like a swallow in its flying, a curse that is causeless does not alight. —Proverbs 26:2

When someone tries to hurt us with their words, the words fly about harmlessly and hurt only the person who spoke them. If we are doing what is right and people talk about it like we are doing something that is evil, then we do not need to pay attention to it. It will not harm us any more than a small bird flying over our head.

—*TNSDB*

August 22

You are a chosen race, a royal priesthood, a holy nation, a people for his own possession, that you may proclaim the excellencies of him who called you out of darkness into his marvelous light. Once you were not a people, but now you are God's people; once you had not received mercy, but now you have received mercy. —1 Peter 2:9-10

Let us remember how the Lord has favored us in his grace. Let everyone among us who is saved remember why he or she is called. We are chosen, royal, priestly, unique, and dearly loved in heaven. How should persons like this behave? We should be far better than others, because the Lord has treated us so much better. May God's rich grace rest on us and cause others to see why our God is worthy of praise.

We were outcast Gentiles who were thought to be little better than dogs. We should be very grateful that we now enjoy the same status as the favored people of old. Lord, cleanse us from all sin and make us devoted to your service. —*TNSDB*

But the fruit of the Spirit is love...against such things there is no law. —Galatians 5:22-23

It speaks in Galatians about love, the fruit of the Spirit being love, joy, peace, patience, kindness, goodness, faithfulness, gentleness, and self-control. The way this writer has put it—and I think it is very beautiful—is that joy is love happy, peace is love at rest, and patience is love enduring. It is all love, you see; gentleness is love in the midst of people, goodness is love in action, faithfulness is love on the battlefield, submissiveness is love at school, and self-control is love in training.

—D. L. Moody, *Christian Love*

Go therefore and make disciples of all nations, baptizing them in the name of the Father and of the Son and of the Holy Spirit. —Matthew 28:19

Oh you heathen, if your religions are true, then why do you not promote them? Gods of heathen, if you are gods, then why do you not command your worshippers to convert the nations to your devotion? But, no, they confess the worthlessness of their system by not having it proclaimed among the nations. When these religions do attempt to spread their message, which is rarely enough, how do they do it? Mohammed put a scimitar into the hand of each of his followers, and said, "That is the strength of Islam; use that sharp argument on the nations." But Christ refused all physical weapons and chose the simple preaching of the word. What other faith can dare to depend on preaching to others one person's testimony about truth that is precious to themselves. Surely this goes to show that the things we believe are powerful, and worthy to be considered with attentive respect.

—Sermon #786 *The Great Mystery of Godliness*

August 25

Jesus said…, "Whoever drinks of the water that I will give him will never be thirsty again." —John 4:14

In that moment when you cast yourself on Christ, Christ comes to you in the living and trustworthy word that lives and continues forever. Though only one drop of the heavenly water of life should drop into your heart, remember this—Jesus, who cannot lie said— "The water that I will give him will become in him a spring of water welling up to eternal life." —Sermon #1850 *Unlimited Love*

August 26

I will not remember your sins.   Isaiah 43:25

Can God forget? Forgetting with God cannot be an impairment like it is with us. We forget because our memory fails, but God forgets in the blessed sense that he remembers the merit of his Son rather than our sins. God forgets sin in the sense that he remembers it is forgiven. I think it was Augustine (who had once been a great sinner) who after he was converted was met in the street by one with whom he had often fallen into sin. When she spoke to him and said, "Augustine, it is I," he said, "Ah, but it is not *I*, I am dead, and made alive again." When God's justice meets a person who believes in Jesus, that person is no longer the *I* that sinned, because that *I* is dead in Christ. —Sermon #1142 *Free Pardon*

Then David came to Nob to Ahimelech the priest. And Ahimelech came to meet David trembling and said to him, "Why are you alone, and no one with you?" —1 Samuel 21:1

Seeing David alone, and obviously in distress, Ahimelech suspected something was wrong.

And David said to Ahimelech the priest, "The king has charged me with a matter and said to me, 'Let no one know anything of the matter about which I send you, and with which I have charged you.'" —1 Samuel 21:2

David spoke falsely and his error is not written here to his honor, but for our warning. This sad falsehood led to terrible results. Oh that good men could always trust in the Lord. —*TNSDB*

There is no hope for anyone to change for the better in the next life. Where death leaves us judgment finds us and eternity holds us.

Now… some of John's disciples…came to John and said to him, "Rabbi, he who was with you across the Jordan, to whom you bore witness—look, he is baptizing, and all are going to him." John answered, "A person cannot receive even one thing unless it is given him from heaven. —John 3:25-27

Each one has his appointed place and John the Baptist had no desire to take over the work of someone else, least of all that of his Lord. The truth stated in this verse should act as an effective cure for envy and wanting more fame than someone else. —*TNSDB*

"I am the LORD your God....Open your mouth wide, and I will fill it." —Psalm 81:10

We are told here to expect great things from God and offer great prayers to him. We will be pleased with the large answers God gives to our large prayers. Who would not ask largely if he believed that God would grant his large requests? God has not set a limit on his promise to hear our prayers. If our answers to our prayers are little, it is because our prayers are little. Come then, let those of us who are believers, beg God for the salvation of the whole family, our relatives and our neighbors. Let our prayers today be very great. Men sin hugely. Let us pray hugely.

"But my people did not listen to my voice....Oh, that my people would listen to me, that Israel would walk in my ways!" —Psalm 81:11a, 13

See the loving tenderness of the Lord. He grieves over our sins because he sees what they cost us. He knows what we lose by our foolishness and he is sorry for us. He does not condemn us with the cold tearless eye of a judge, but as a father who scolds with a loving sadness in his heart. —*TNSDB*

Where is the one who is wise? Where is the scribe? Where is the debater of this age? Has not God made foolish the wisdom of the world? —1 Corinthians 1:20

Never forget this. It will help cure us of wishing for the world's idea of scholarly and intellectual preaching. Why should we want what God intends to destroy? The plain gospel of Jesus, simply preached, is infinitely superior to all the "deep thinking" and supposed "scientific reasoning" of modern times. —*TNSDB*

Knock, and it will be opened to you. —Matthew 7:7

When people can be let in by knocking, a door knocker is usually placed on the door. Otherwise, we often see the words NO ADMITTANCE. Before doorbells became so common the habit of knocking at the door was almost universal and people were accustomed to make the door boom with their blows. There was a strike plate (or nailhead) for the knocker to drop on. People used to strike it so heavily that some said the blows were killing. That is where the amusing proverb, "As dead as a door nail" came from. It indicates a wholehearted kind of knocking, the kind I would have you imitate in prayer. Knock at heaven's gate as intensely as people knocked at doors in the olden days. Have you not had knocks at your own doors that could be heard throughout the house? Some of our friends are vigorous and knock as if they meant to come in. It may be that gentle folks give such tender taps that no one in the house can hear them, and so they have to wait. But the ones I am talking about never fall into that error, because they startle everyone so much that people are glad to let them in, for fear they should thunder a second time. Pray that way. Let us plead downright earnestly and never stop until we gain entrance.

—Sermon #1723 *Knock*

Expect great things from God. Attempt great things for God.
—*William Carey (1793-1834). Baptist missionary to India.*

SEPTEMBER 1

"THESE ARE HARD TIMES!"

Times have always been hard ever since I can remember and I suppose they always will be. They used to be hard in our grandfathers' days and it seems there is every chance they will continue that way. Yet we always talk about "the good old days." When our children are our age, they will talk about our times as "the good old days" too. The fact is, right now is the best time that ever was, and *now* is the only time that belongs to us. The past is gone and the future is yet to be. We live in the present; let us make the proper use of it. —Sermon #440 *Cheer for the Fainthearted*

Have we lived in such a way that the poor would rejoice to see us back again when we die?

SEPTEMBER 2

THE FIRST ADAM LOOKED on the tree and plucked its fruit and fell. The second Adam was nailed to the tree. "Cursed is everyone who is hanged on a tree." He became a curse for us. The two marvelous events that have taken place in the world are these, that when the first Adam went up from Eden he left a curse on the earth, but when the second Adam went up from the Mount of Olives he lifted the curse. The first brought the curse on the earth, the second as he went up from the Mount of Olives lifted the curse, and so every person that is in Christ can shout Victory! and there is no victory until they are in Christ. —D. L. Moody, *The Two Adams*

SEPTEMBER 3

The time of the promise. —Acts 7:17a

Perhaps we have not yet displayed enough submission to the divine will. Patience has not yet had its full effect. The process of bringing our will in line with God's will is not finished. We are still craving after the comforts that the Lord intends for us to completely outgrow. Leave your idols; forsake those things you desire and adore; and the promised peace will come to you.

—According to Promise

Blessed be his name. He does not forget us
like we so easily forget him.

SEPTEMBER 4

WHEN KING SOLOMON BEGAN WORK ON
A HOUSE FOR THE NAME OF THE LORD

At the king's command they quarried out great, costly stones in order to lay the foundation of the house with dressed stones.

—1 Kings 5:17

Even the foundation stones were not rugged and rough, but cut and expensive. God would have everything that is done for him done well. He does not care so much for that which pleases the eye of man; his delight is with the beauty of those living stones of his spiritual temple that are hidden from view. *—TNSDB*

Whoever winks the eye causes trouble, but a babbling fool will come to ruin. —Proverbs 10:10

Cowards are afraid to say things they know they should not, but express their feelings with a clever wink of the eye. They cause much misery. No true man will behave that way.

People who talk too much prove that their religion is not real. Their profession of faith will soon become a shipwreck. —*TNSDB*

Your arrows have sunk into me, and your hand has come down on me. —*Psalm 38:2*

God disciplines many of his children severely, yet still loves them, and will not suppress his mercy forever. —*Thomas Wilcocks (1549-1608)*

For the LORD God is a sun and shield;
the LORD bestows favor and honor.
No good thing does he withhold
from those who walk uprightly. —Psalm 84:11

What a great promise, or rather, what a great set of promises! Here we have all we need for all time and for all eternity. What an encouragement to pray! If all things are freely given to us by God, then let us open our mouths wide when making our requests. What more can God himself say than he has said in this most precious verse? —*TNSDB*

Rescue me. —Psalm 35:17

Satan no sooner sees us wandering from the path of righteousness, but he quickly runs to God in protest, filling out complaints against us in the courtroom of heaven. The matter would go hard on us, except for the Great Lord Chancellor of peace, our Advocate Jesus Christ. As God puts our tears in his bottle, and keeps track of the very groans of our holy suffering in a book, so Satan keeps a record of our sins, and sues for justice against us. If God were like a human, subject to emotions, or easily swayed by the suggestions of the common attorney, then heartache awaits us. But he will listen to one son of truth before ten thousand fathers of lies. It makes no difference what libel the plaintiff presents, when the judge acquits. We have forfeited our positions through treason, and the busy devil accuses us; but there is no proof, because one steps in, and pleads a former ruling, a rule involving both promise and purchase. "*Lord..., rescue my soul from their destructions, my darling from the lions.*" Lord Jesus, claim your own; do not let Satan win by force or fraud, what you have bought with your own blood. —Thomas Adams (1701-1784)

Solomon answered all [the queen of Sheba's] questions; there was nothing hidden from the king that he could not explain to her. —1 Kings 10:3

When sinners come to Jesus they will find solutions to all their difficult questions. He will both reveal and remove all their secret uneasiness. He is always ready to share his wisdom to all who come to him. There will never be a situation that he cannot work out. —*TNSDB*

I will not remember your sins. —Isaiah 43:25

A human being might pardon an offense against him, but not know the full extent of the offense. They might soon wake up to a fuller sense of the offense committed against them and feel new anger at the offender. A king can only forgive a rebel for the acts of which he knows he is guilty. The Lord knows all our sins. There is not a sin that has ever escaped his eyes. He knows those committed in secret, in the darkness of the night. He knows those that never struggled into action, sins of the heart and imagination that are known only to you and God. What does he not see? This is a blessing for us, because it means our pardon covers the full extent of our sin.

—Sermon #1142 *Free Pardon*

Jesus was led up by the Spirit into the wilderness to be tempted by the devil. —*Matthew 4:1*

The first Adam was tempted by his bride.

The second was tempted for his bride. —*D. L. Moody The Two Adams*

To the one who knocks it will be opened. —Matthew 7:8

At a Primitive Methodist meeting someone was trying to pray, but could not get the words out. And then a voice was heard from the corner of the room, "Plead the blood, brother! Plead the blood!" I am not very fond of such interruptions, but this was commendable, because it gave sound advice and put the person praying on solid ground. Plead the precious blood of Jesus Christ and you have knocked in a way that must be heard.

—Sermon #1723 *Knock*

For to the one who has, more will be given, and he will have an abundance. —Matthew 13:12

If you are struggling with unbelief, be willing to believe what you can believe. Make it your desire to believe. Dear friend, if you cannot yet follow the Lord into the depths, he will save you if you follow him into the shallows as far as you can. If a truth confuses you, do not make that an excuse for rejecting your Lord, but be willing to accept what does not confuse you. If you cannot seem to reach his divine person, then at least touch the fringe of his garment. You will soon discover that your faith in the basic truths of the gospel will, by the grace of the Holy Spirit, lead you to an understanding of the deeper mysteries. Use your starlight and you shall soon have sunlight. —Sermon #1488 *More & More, or Less & Less*

The devil comes and takes away the word from their hearts.
—Luke 8:12

The power of the evil one springs mainly from our own evil. Let us ask the Lord to renew our hearts so the gospel of Jesus may be accepted wholeheartedly and may never be taken away. The need for this kind of prayer is great. Our adversary is no imaginary being. His existence is real, his presence constant, his power immense, and his activity tireless. Lord, match him and outmatch him. Drive away this foulest of fowls, this most disgusting of birds. Break up the soil of the soul. Let your truth truly live and graciously grow with us.

—Sermon #1459 *Satan's Punctuality, Power, and Purpose*

Faith comes from hearing, and hearing through the word of Christ. —Romans 10:17

Satan's method for preventing faith is to destroy the word, to remove all trace of it. Here is another practical lesson to be learned from the devil's tactics. Let us keep the gospel near the mind of the unconverted as much as possible. Let us sow and sow again, in the hope that some grain may take root. Farmers in the country were in the habit, when planting certain seeds, to put in "one for the worm, and one for the crow, and then a third which would surely grow," and we must do the same.

—Sermon #1459 *Satan's Punctuality, Power, and Purpose*

When I spoke to you persistently you did not listen, and when I called you, you did not answer. —Jeremiah 7:13

Surely, if the Lord himself continued to speak like this to an unresponsive nation, we should not grumble if much of our preaching seems to be useless. There is life in the seed of the gospel and it will grow if it can be put into the soil of the heart. Therefore, let us have faith in it and never dream of obtaining a crop except by the old-fashioned way of sowing good seed. The devil obviously hates the word, so let us treasure it, and sow it everywhere. —Sermon #1459 *Satan's Punctuality, Power, and Purpose*

SEPTEMBER 15

WHEN ISRAEL WENT OUT TO BATTLE AGAINST THE PHILISTINES AND BROUGHT THE ARK OF THE COVENANT OF THE LORD INTO THE CAMP

"Take courage, and be men, O Philistines, lest you become slaves to the Hebrews as they have been to you; be men and fight." —1 Samuel 4:9

The Philistines were heathens and thought the ark was God himself. However, they were correct in thinking that if God was on Israel's side, it would not go well with them. If they had understood that God is Almighty, they would not have attempted to fight against him. But they thought Jehovah was like their own god, Dagon, who had only limited powers. Therefore they showed their bravery by deciding to fight like true soldiers. If these Philistines could be so bold in what appeared to be a hopeless situation, how brave should we be who have the assurance of victory, because the Lord of Hosts is with us? Our Lord says to us, "Take courage, and be men." To be cowardly in the cause of Jesus would be disgraceful! Never let the fear of man have the slightest power over you. Do not doubt the reality of the power of your Lord. —*TNSDB*

SEPTEMBER 16

They did not destroy the peoples, as the LORD commanded them. —Psalms 106:34

This was the Jews main sin. All of their other faults were a result of not obeying this command. They were brought to Canaan to destroy the criminal nations that lived there. Israel was either too afraid or too rebellious to finish the job. As a result, more sin and sorrow followed their first sin. No one can fully understand how much evil may follow one act of disobedience. If we allow just one sin to be out of control, it will become a terrible plague in our life. Oh for grace to make careful work of removing such sin. Only the Holy Spirit can help us in doing this. —*TNSDB*

September 17

Abram said to the king of Sodom, "I have lifted my hand to the LORD, God Most High, Possessor of heaven and earth, that I would not take...anything that is yours, lest you should say, 'I have made Abram rich.'"

—Genesis 14:22-23

The king of Sodom offered Abram what was rightfully his by the laws of war, but he refused to take it. Sometimes the right thing to do is give up what is rightfully ours. Abram believed God could give him all he needed without owing the king of Sodom a debt of gratitude. Faith does not look for man to provide. She will not give the world the opportunity to say, "See we provided for you, not God. You should praise us, not the Lord." Jehovah is more than enough for believers. We do not need to depend on anyone else.

—*TNSDB*

September 18

The tendency of the awakened mind is to dwell on the dark side of God's word and feel the full force of it. At the same time the brighter portion of the Bible is neglected, as though it was too good to be true. This is foolishness. If we measure every blessing by our unworthiness, then they are all too good for us. But, if we evaluate the blessings by God's outstanding excellence, then no blessing is too good for God to give. It is the nature of a God of love to give limitless blessing. If Alexander the Great gave like a king, will Jehovah not give like a God? —*According to Promise*

The old has passed away; behold, the new has come.

—2 Corinthians 5:17

You should try to learn from those who have been in the church a long time. If you take my advice you will select your friends from experienced Christians. You must keep in the company of people who know more than yourself. That's the way I do. Of course, I get the best of the bargain that way, but that is what you want; you can learn something from them and will not be mixing with the ungodly and the unconverted. You do not need to become like ungodly people when you happen to be thrown together with them; you can be in the world and not be of the world.

Not only that, but what you want is to get in love with this blessed Bible; and the moment you get full of Bible truths, the world has lost its power. Then you won't be saying, "Do I have to give up this? Do I have to give up that?" You never hear Bible Christians talk like that. There are some things I used to like to do before I was converted that I don't do now; but thank God, I don't want to do them. God has turned my appetite against such things. I have been fed on this blessed Bible until I no longer have any taste for the books I used to like.

—D. L. Moody, *Message to Young Converts*

He laid down his life for us. —1 John 3:16a

Come, believer, and examine this majestic truth, proclaimed to you in simple monosyllables. "He laid down his life for us." There is not one long word in this statement; it is all as simple as it can be; and it is simple because it is so grand. Inspiring thoughts always need simplicity in words to express themselves. Little thoughts require great words to explain them; little preachers need complex words to communicate their feeble ideas, but great thoughts and the great champions of those thoughts are content with little words.

—Sermon #2656 *The Death of Christ for His People*

SEPTEMBER 21

In everything…let your requests be made known to God.

—Philippians 4:6

If any child of God wants God to speak words of comfort to them, they must speak to God in prayer. If you want to have the witness of the Holy Spirit in your soul, then "In everything…let your requests be made known to God." Do not neglect the throne of grace. —Sermon # 909 *Voices From the Excellent Glory*

SEPTEMBER 22

So Sarah laughed to herself…. But Sarah denied it, saying, "I did not laugh," for she was afraid. [The LORD] said, "No, but you did laugh." —Genesis 18:12, 15

He who knows all hearts cannot be deceived. See how honest Holy Scripture is, it records the faults of even the best of the saints. See also how tender the Spirit of God is, because in the New Testament Sarah's fault is not mentioned. It had been forgiven and blotted out, but the fact that she called her husband "lord" is recorded to her honor. We serve a gracious God who, when our hearts are right, commends our good fruit, and leaves the unripe figs to drop out of sight [a reference to Revelation 6:13]. Let us be careful not to spoil the joy of his promises and grace by any improper words or actions. It would be a sad thing for us to be surrounded by the memories of divine love and have to admit that we laughed at the promise. —*TNSDB*

And Lot lifted up his eyes and saw that the Jordan Valley was well watered everywhere like the garden of the LORD.... So Lot chose for himself all the Jordan Valley.... Thus they separated from each other. Abram settled in the land of Canaan, while Lot settled among the cities of the valley and moved his tent as far as Sodom. Now the men of Sodom were wicked, great sinners against the LORD.

—Genesis 13:10-13

Lot made a serious mistake. He looked only to the richness of the country and not to the character of the people. He walked by sight and not by faith. He looked at the material advantage and did not "seek first the kingdom of God" (Matthew 6:33). Lot gave up living a life of separation to live in the city. He was influenced by the residents of Sodom and became worldly. He gave up all claim to the inheritance promised to Abram and his descendants and pierced himself through with many sorrows. In the end, the person who wanted everything the world had to offer lost it and the person who was willing to give up anything to honor God found it.

When friends leave us, we may expect the Lord to visit us with comfort and support. After Lot was gone, the Lord appeared again to Abraham. —*TNSDB*

By faith [Abraham] went to live in the land of promise, as in a foreign land, living in tents with Isaac and Jacob, heirs with him of the same promise. he was looking forward to the city that has foundations, whose designer and builder is God.

—Hebrews 11:9-10

Abraham had to leave idolatrous Chaldea. We must also separate ourselves from a world that is controlled by the wicked one. He understood he was like an outsider in this temporary life and we must too. This world is not our home where we can relax. Ours is the life of a traveler until we reach "the city that has foundations." Abraham pitched his tent and wandered up and down in the land as a stranger, not as a citizen of Canaan. We do not have a permanent city here, but we look for one in the future. He who finds a place to rest here does not have one in heaven.

—TNSDB

SEPTEMBER 25

As a father shows compassion to his children, so the LORD shows compassion to those who fear him. —Psalm 103:13

That is, he grieves with, is affected by, feels for, and sympathizes with them in all of their afflictions. It is a great thing for a lowly person to have the compassion of the great and mighty, but for a lowly sinner to be in the heart and affections of God, this is astonishing to consider. Yet, this is the case for those who fear God! —John Bunyan, *The Fear of God*

SEPTEMBER 26

To believe that God will give us something he has never promised to give, is no more than dreaming. Faith must have a promise either implied or clearly stated in the Bible or it is a reckless faith. Even if our trust should cry itself hoarse in prayer, it would still be no more than the ranting of someone who had lost their mind, if it did not have the Word of God to support it. Thankfully, the promises and truths revealed in the Scripture are more than enough for every real emergency. But when uncontrolled gullibility takes hold of every urge of its own crazy imagination, and hopes to see it come true, then disappointment should not surprise us. It is our duty to believe the certain things in God's revelation to us, but we are not to waste a grain of precious faith on anything outside of that circle.

—The Clue of the Maze

FAITH AND ITS EARLY ANXIETIES

Our persistent unbelief ends when we see God as he is revealed in the Bible and reach complete confidence in him. However, fits of doubt are likely to sneak up on us without warning. Are they not like a seizure of the mind? Belief in the great unseen God is not natural to the flesh, which still craves for signs and wonders that the eyes can see. It is common for young believers to be weak on their feet. The memory of past sin and the sense of present weakness may cause this feeling of inadequacy in the spiritually young. The strangeness and greatness of spiritual discoveries may strike them with fear. But let them hold on to faith in God with a death grip and the darkness will disappear. —*The Clue of the Maze*

One Thing Is Necessary —Luke 10:42

In these days of rapid transportation and modern communication, we cannot get time to listen to Christ whispering in our ears. We are so busy we do not choose that one thing necessary. If we did, we would not talk so much as we would listen, and when we did speak it would be only when we had something to say. We would hear words that came from the Master, and they would burn down deep into our souls and produce fruit. —D. L. Moody Sermon: *The Six "One Things"*

SEPTEMBER 29

"For the bread of God is he who comes down from heaven and gives life to the world." They said to him, "Sir, give us this bread always." —John 6:33-34

Some asked in honest ignorance, expecting Jesus to supply them with food everyday for nothing. But others only said this to insult him and make fun of him. If the Lord would give them bread the rest of their lives, then they would believe he was the Messiah, but not unless he did. But without meaning to, these unbelievers have provided us with a prayer we can use every hour. It is full of meaning and exactly expresses our need and our desire. Let us carry it with us all this day as our heart's wish and prayer: "Lord, give us this bread always." —*TNSDB*

SEPTEMBER 30

So Jesus said to them, "Truly, truly, I say to you, unless you eat the flesh of the Son of Man and drink his blood, you have no life in you." —John 6:53

He was not referring to the Lord's Supper. It had not been established yet and it is not absolutely necessary for salvation. The dying thief did not receive a sacrament and yet he was with his Lord in Paradise as soon as he died. The eating and drinking Jesus talked about here is spiritual and only those who have been born again can have a part in them. These words of Jesus search the heart. Multitudes of people who profess to be Christians have no personal experience of this spiritual feeding that our Lord meant. Involvement in the person and work of Jesus leads to a lasting joining with him, and a close and dear fellowship with him. This truth cannot be repeated too often. Eternal life can only be ours as we accept the incarnate God by faith and make him the life of our soul. —*TNSDB*

OCTOBER 1

They have rejected the word of the LORD, so what wisdom is in them? —Jeremiah 8:9

Those who do not respect the Word of the Lord, those who do not dread and fear it, but allow the desires of the flesh, the desires of the eyes, and the pride in possessions to rule their lives, are sharply rebuked by this teaching. They are considered the fools of the world. That such people exist is obvious, not only by their unstable lives, but by the clear testimony of the Word. "As for the word that you have spoken to us in the name of the LORD," they said to Jeremiah, "we will not listen to you. But we will do everything that we have vowed" (Jeremiah 44:16-17). Was this only the rage of wicked men back then? Is there not the same spirit of rebellion with us today? Without question it is so, because there is nothing new. "What has been is what will be, and what has been done is what will be done, and there is nothing new under the sun" (Ecclesiastes 1:9). Therefore, as it was then, it is with many in this day. —John Bunyan, *The Fear of God*

OCTOBER 2

THERE IS NOTHING UNREASONABLE IN HUMBLY BELIEVING GOD

Daring to question God's word, however, is anything but reasonable. We are not likely to make a mistake in trusting the promise too much. Our failure lies in lack of faith, not in too much. It would be hard to believe God too much. It is all too common to believe him too little. "According to your faith be it done to you," is a blessing from which the Lord will never back away. "If you can, all things are possible for one who believes." It is written, "They were unable to enter because of unbelief," but it is never said that someone who entered in by faith was criticized for their rudeness and driven out. —According to Promise

OCTOBER 3

Now the word of the LORD came to Jonah the son of Amittai, saying, "Arise, go to Nineveh, that great city, and call out against it, for their evil has come up before me." —Jonah 1:1-2

Nineveh has been described as being protected by a 60 mile wall surrounding the city and 1,000,000 people living in it. It was full of idols and its wealth was acquired by attacking and stealing from other nations. It was very gracious on the Lord's part to send a prophet to warn such a city. But it was no small task for one man to take on such an unwelcome assignment.

But Jonah rose to flee to Tarshish from the presence of the LORD. —Jonah 1:3

Who would have thought that a prophet would act so wickedly? "Let anyone who thinks that he stands take heed lest he fall" (1 Corinthians 10:12). We are much weaker than a prophet and more likely to fall. Therefore let us pray to the Lord to keep us from falling. —*TNSDB*

OCTOBER 4

[Jonah] went down to Joppa and found a ship going to Tarshish. —Jonah 1:4a

Some would think that Jonah finding a ship ready to sail away from his assignment was actually arranged by God so he would not need to follow the Lord's express command. Old Thomas Adams (1583-1652) says, "If you will flee from God, the devil will loan you both spurs and a horse. Yes, a ready horse that will carry you swiftly." It is our duty to follow God's orders and not the apparent leading of circumstances.

So he paid the fare and went on board, to go with them to Tarshish, away from the presence of the LORD. —Jonah 1:4b

Sin is expensive. A price must be paid. People will grumble about any little amount they are asked to give for the cause of God, but they do not care how much they have to pay to satisfy their wrong desires. Jonah took on a foolish mission when he tried to run away from the Lord. God is everywhere. He is just as present in Tarshish as in Nineveh! —*TNSDB*

OCTOBER 5

Then [the mariners] said to [Jonah], "What shall we do to you, that the sea may quiet down for us?" For the sea grew more and more tempestuous. —Jonah 1:8

The sailors were reluctant to lift up their hands against Jonah. They were afraid to injure him even though he was clearly guilty. They did not even insult him, as some would have done. Let us learn from this to never be harsh with our brothers and sisters in Christ, even if their faults result in trouble and great danger for us. Instead, let us allow them to condemn themselves and suggest what steps should be taken to correct the situation. —*TNSDB*

OCTOBER 6

WHEN GOD RELENTED OF THE DISASTER THAT HE HAD SAID HE WOULD DO TO NINEVEH

But it displeased Jonah exceedingly, and he was angry. And he prayed to the LORD and said, "O LORD, is not this what I said when I was yet in my country? That is why I made haste to flee to Tarshish; for I knew that you are a gracious God and merciful, slow to anger and abounding in steadfast love, and relenting from disaster. Therefore now, O LORD, please take my life from me, for it is better for me to die than to live."

—Jonah 4:1-3

We cannot love Jonah when we see him so irritable, but we must remember that he wrote this himself. He paints his own portrait in the blackest colors and does not try to excuse or explain away his gloomy temper. He was a man of serious integrity. He was extremely sensitive about being completely truthful about his personal character. He was afraid his reputation would be tarnished, so he fell into a very bad mood. A good man should not mope about like this. —*TNSDB*

OCTOBER 7

Let those who delight in my righteousness shout for joy and be glad. —Psalm 35:27

See how the hearts of the saints have joined ranks against their persecutors. The saints still have access to the weapon of prayer in times of persecution. When the Romans were up against it, they were glad to take the weapons out of the temples of their gods to fight against their enemies—and they were victorious! So, when the people of God are hard pressed due to afflictions and persecutions, the weapons they flee to are prayers and tears; and with these have overcome their persecutors.

—Thomas Brooks (1608-1680)

All church work will be done when each of us works diligently to accomplish the job the Lord has given them.

OCTOBER 8

The Spirit of God is still with us, working through the word of God. See the savage throwing down his weapons, look on the cannibal softened into the man. What philosophy could not do or even care to attempt, what civilization could never have accomplished alone, the cross of Christ has successfully performed. The Spirit of God is with us. He is seen in both the holiness of the saints and in the conversions of unbelievers. He gives his testimony that God was in Christ.

— Sermon #786 *The Great Mystery of Godliness*

You say that you have been upstairs to pray, but you have gained no comfort from it. Let me suggest that, the next time you go upstairs, you sing a psalm. "Oh, I have been up and down," says one, "trying to get excited and dedicated about praying." May I also suggest to you that you stop that method, for a while, and begin to praise God? How often do you praise God during the day? I think you do get alone to pray, and you would be ashamed if you did not do so once, twice, or three or even more times during the day; but how often do you praise God?

Now, you know that you will not pray in heaven—it will be all praise there. So, do not neglect that necessary part of your education which is "Raise a song" here and now.

—Sermon #2679 *Christ's Indwelling Word*

OCTOBER 10

John said to him, "Teacher, we saw someone casting out demons in your name, and we tried to stop him, because he was not following us." —Mark 9:38

John thought that anyone who was not in complete agreement with them must be stopped and his fellow apostles shared the feeling. They had all the zeal of denominations that think only they have the truth and that all others are not truly Christian. This unknown worker honored the name of Jesus and demonstrated the Lord's power. One would have thought that the apostles would have recognized him as a brother. But no, "He was not following us" was enough to sour all their brotherly kindness. They tried to stop the good man from casting out any more devils, or do anything more in the name of Jesus. This was an example of *church*ianity, but it was not *Christ*ianity. —*TNSDB*

OCTOBER 11

THE MAN WHOSE SON HAD AN UNCLEAN SPIRIT

And Jesus said to him, "If you can! All things are possible for one who believes." —Mark 9:23

The Savior puts the responsibility for the unbelieving "if you can" where it belonged. The lack of power never lies in Jesus, but in our faith.

Immediately the father of the child cried out and said, "I believe; help my unbelief! —Mark 9:24

Here is a prayer that is most appropriate for many struggling believers, in whom faith and unbelief are battling for control.

—TNSDB

When we honor God the most, he will be ready to help the most.

OCTOBER 12

I will thank you forever,
because you have done it.
I will wait for your name, for it is good,
in the presence of the godly. —Psalm 52:9

David's thankfulness was always there, just like the mercy he rejoiced in. He looked on God's punishment of his enemies as if it had already happened: "You have done it." Therefore he waited patiently until the bright days should dawn for himself and the persecuted church. He believed, as we also should, that he should wait quietly for the Lord to act in his own good time. It is good for the Lord's saints to act this way. It is also a good way to encourage our fellow believers. Patiently waiting on the Lord helps us to keep our souls at peace. *—TNSDB*

OCTOBER 13

I would not be surprised if those Israelites who were born in the wilderness, and had gathered manna every morning for years, had stopped marveling at it, or no longer saw the hand of the Lord in it. Shameful stupidity! But, oh, how common! Many people have lived from hand to mouth, and seen the hand of the Lord in the gift of every mouthful of food; at last, by God's goodness, they have prospered in this world, and earned a regular income, which they received without concern or trouble. But they soon came to look at it as the natural result of their own efforts, and no longer praised the loving-kindness of the Lord. —*According to Promise*

When we are at the end of having our own way,
we are not far away from the end of our trials.

OCTOBER 14

Now God is just what he says he is, and he wants his children to be sincere in love; not to love just merely in word and in talk, but to love in earnest. That is what God does. You ask me why God loves. You might as well ask me why the sun shines. It can't help shining, and neither can God help loving, because he is love himself, and anyone that says he is not love does not know anything about love. If "God's love has been poured into our hearts," we will show it in our lives. We will not have to go up and down the earth proclaiming it. We will show it in everything we say or do. —D. L. Moody, *Christian Love*

For if they fall, one will lift up his fellow. —Ecclesiastes 4:10

What is the lesson here? Why, perhaps the faith of some of you here tonight is so strong that you hardly know what to do with it. What should you do? If someone sitting in the seat behind you is fainting, and you have some strong smelling salts, you would pass them over. Now sometimes our faith is intended to be used like those ammonia inhalants. If you are strong, then help your weak brother or sister in the Lord. If you see any struggling, then lift them on your shoulders—help to carry them. Does not your Master carry the lambs on his shoulders? Imitate him, and sometimes carry a lamb on your shoulders too. It is a divine thing to wipe tears from all eyes. Perhaps your faith is meant to be a handkerchief with which you may wipe away the tears of your brother or sister. Help to hold up your trembling friend for a while. It may be that in some brighter day with them, when you are experiencing a dark hour, they will repay you with interest for the little cheer you give them today.

—Sermon #440 *Cheer for the Fainthearted*

When Hezekiah Welcomed the Envoys of the King of Babylon and Showed Them All His Treasures
—2 Kings 20:12-13

At first sight this looks harmless enough, but the Lord saw that the king was proud, delighted in the flatteries of heathen strangers, and perhaps hoped to strengthen himself by associating with their expanding kingdom. God is jealous over those he loves. His strictness with them is in proportion to his love for them. This sad fault of good Hezekiah led a godly writer [Joseph Hall (1574-1656)] to cry, "Oh God! If you do not keep us as well in our sunshine as in our storm, we are sure to perish. During our times of tribulation and during our times of wealth, good Lord, deliver us!" —*TNSDB*

So Jotham became mighty, because he ordered his ways before the LORD his God. —2 Chronicles 27:6

He was careful and thoughtful in the way he lived his life. He also feared sinning unintentionally. This made him strong. There is a great deal of meaning in the words, "He ordered his ways before the Lord his God." They imply that he was not a follower of men or cared about their praise, but that he lived like he was always in the presence of the Lord and wanted more than anything else to please him. —*TNSDB*

God watches me all the time.
Whether I am awake or asleep, his eye is on me!

WHEN KING JEROBOAM MADE TWO CALVES OF GOLD
AND SAID TO THE PEOPLE,

"Behold your gods." —1 Kings 12:28

People naturally love things that require little effort. They prefer a religion that will not trouble them or interrupt their lives very much. That is the reason Jeroboam appealed to the shameful tendencies of their human nature. But how disgraceful it was for Israel to forsake the living God and bow before the image of a bull just as an excuse to not have to travel so far. May we never leave the good old paths of truth because it would be convenient, or give us a better chance of advancement in our job or better opportunities to make more money. Let us hold tightly to the Lord with all our heart. —*TNSDB*

OCTOBER 19

He who quarries stones is hurt by them, and he who splits logs is endangered by them. —Ecclesiastes 10:9

There is some risk in any kind of job. This is a good reason to ask the Lord to keep us safe every day, however free from danger our work may seem to be. —*TNSDB*

If we go only where God directs us, and keep away from where he gives us no permission to be, our journey will be a great success.

OCTOBER 20

He knows the way that I take; when he has tried me, I shall come out as gold. —Job 23:10

This confidence is based on the Lord's knowledge of us. "He knows the way that I take," therefore, "When he has tried me, I will come out as gold." If something could happen to us that the Lord had not foreseen and provided for, we might be in great danger. But he knows our way even to the finish and has prepared for the rough places. If some amazing calamity could come upon us on which the Lord had not counted, we might well be afraid of being shipwrecked. But our Lord's foreseeing eye has swept the horizon and prepared us for all weathers. He knows where storms lie in wait and cyclones hide. He is at home managing tempests and tornadoes. If his farseeing eye has spied out a long sickness for us and a gradual and painful death, then he has prepared whatever is necessary to take us through it. If he has looked into the mysterious unknown of the apocalyptic revelation and seen unimaginable horrors and terrors that would melt the heart, he has already anticipated and prepared for them. It is enough for us that our Father knows what we need and that, "When he has tried us, we will come out as gold." —Sermon #2098 *Where Are You Going?*

YOU MUST BE BORN AGAIN

That which is born of the flesh is flesh, and that which is born of the Spirit is spirit. —John 3:6

Flesh at its best can only produce flesh. Since we must become spiritual to enter the spiritual kingdom of Jesus, it is obvious that we must be born again or else remain strangers to the things of God. Every person must be born twice or die twice. Let us never forget this. —*TNSDB*

Under that old dispensation of the law it was do and live —now it is live and do. —D.L. Moody Abounding Grace.

THE WOMAN AT THE WELL

They went out of the town and were coming to [Jesus].
—John 4:30

God blessed the woman's testimony so that the curiosity of the people of the town was excited. She had become a link in the chain of events that led to the conversion of many. We might all be useful if we would only try. —*TNSDB*

Then my soul will rejoice in the LORD, exulting in his salvation. —Psalm 35:9

As a result of being rescued, David gives all the honor to the Judge of the just. He does not brag about his own courage. He turns from his enemies to his God, and finds a deep, unbroken joy in Jehovah; his spirit celebrates his Lord. We do not rejoice in the destruction of others, but in the salvation that God gives to us. Answered prayer should always lead to praise. It would be good if we were more open and expressive in our holy rejoicing. We rob God by suppressing grateful emotions. —*The Treasury of David*

We may not have been the worst of men,
but we are sorry that there should be any worse than we are.

Search me, O God. —Psalm 139:23

When we think that we are getting over some particular temptation, it is at that point that it is overcoming us. When you suppose that you are the master of that temptation, it has probably mastered you. Come, brothers and sisters, we had better quit that foolish thinking. This person, whom we are trying to search, is much too deep for us. I mean, that we are so ready to fool ourselves, that we cannot discover our true selves. Instead, let us pray to the Lord, "Search me, O God, and know my heart! Try me and know my thoughts! And see if there be any grievous way in me, and lead me in the way everlasting!"

—Sermon #2844 *The Seed on Rocky Ground*

OCTOBER 25

There was no water for the people to drink. Therefore the people quarreled with Moses and said, "Give us water to drink." And Moses said to them, "Why do you quarrel with me? Why do you test the LORD?" —Exodus 17:1-2

God's people never go long before they are tested. Complaining about things that happen to us is really complaining about the Lord, no matter how we may try to hide it. After all, what did Moses have to do with it? The source of this sin of grumbling was unbelief. Could they not trust Jehovah? Would he not be sure to supply their needs? Had he ever forgotten them? In spite of all our experience of God's faithfulness to us, we are also guilty of the sin of not believing our Lord. He who is without fault among us, let him throw the first stone at Israel. —*TNSDB*

OCTOBER 26

So they gave a dinner for [Jesus] there. Martha served, and Lazarus was one of those reclining with him at the table.
—John 12:2

Christ had once reproved Martha for being "distracted with much serving," but we find her still serving. She had not taken the rebuke incorrectly and she had not become oversensitive and quit serving altogether, as some would have done. She loved her Lord too much for that. This time she served within hearing of the Lord's gracious words. She served without complaining or being upset. It is good when good people grow better. Lazarus was highly favored and yet his situation was only the same as all whom the Lord gives new life. Those who are made alive by him are those who sit together with him. —*TNSDB*

THE LORD'S MOTIVES FOR FORGIVING SIN

Brothers and sisters, the Lord knows his motives for pardoning sinners and it is not for us to judge them. But, first, is it not so he can take pleasure in his mercy? Of all God's attributes, he uses mercy last, but it is the one that pleases him most. The Lord blots out sin, because he is full of mercy. Another motive is to glorify his Son, who is one with the Father. His Son has made atonement. He has offered and presented it. And now, so that he may have his full reward, the Lord delights to blot out the sins of those who come to him. The motive lies in God himself. What a comfort this is. If I look into my soul, I cannot see any reason why God should save me. But I do not need to be concerned, because the motive lies in our gracious God alone. —Sermon #1142 *Free Pardon*

To confess that you were wrong yesterday,
is only to acknowledge that you are a little wiser today.

I have no greater joy than to hear that my children are walking in the truth. —3 John 4

John loved his converts like they were his own children. He was glad when he found them correct in doctrine and practice. What would he say about the doubting of many in the church today? It would break the good man's heart. God's people should hold on to the truth more firmly than ever, because many, including many church attendees, idolize clever skepticism. —*TNSDB*

October 29

Religion that is pure and undefiled before God, the Father, is this: to visit orphans and widows in their affliction, and to keep oneself unstained from the world.

—James 1:27

These are the best kinds of outward worship. They are the distinctive signs of divine living. The more visiting and praying at sick beds, and help received by orphans, the better. Let us remember these today and help to support them. —*TNSDB*

Editor's Note: In Spurgeon's day children of destitute mothers, who had no means to support them, were accepted into orphanages (including those founded by Spurgeon).

October 30

We have this as a sure and steadfast anchor of the soul, a hope that enters into the inner place behind the curtain, where Jesus has gone as a forerunner on our behalf, having become a high priest forever after the order of Melchizedek.

—Hebrews 6:19-20

We are given the most serious warnings against abandoning the faith and the declaration that total desertion would be fatal (Hebrews 6:4-8). Does this contradict the great truth that all true saints are eternally safe? No! They are safe because of the covenant promise and God's oath guaranteeing their security. Their hope is placed where it cannot fail. Jesus has gone, in their name, to take possession of heaven. Has he gone on ahead on behalf of people who will perish along the way? God forbid! Where our Head is now, the members of his body must be before long. —*TNSDB*

HOPE AND FEAR

There are two things that motivate people in this life, HOPE and FEAR. Fear comes from fixing our attention on the threats and fearful judgments of God; as being a God in whose sight no one is clean, everyone is a sinner, everyone is damnable. But hope comes from fixing our attention on the promises, and the all-sweet mercies of God; as it is written, "Remember your mercy, O LORD, and your steadfast love, for they have been from of old" (Psalm 25:6). Between these two, as between the upper and lower millstone, we must always be ground, and kept, so that we never turn either to the right hand or to the left. Trying to escape is the condition familiar to hypocrites, who are motivated by two contrary things, security and headstrong confidence.

—Martin Luther (1483-1546)

NOVEMBER 1

As you received Christ Jesus the Lord, so walk in him, rooted and built up in him and established in the faith, just as you were taught, abounding in thanksgiving.

—Colossians 2:6-7

May the Lord allow us to do so. The gospel that has saved us is also good enough to live by and to die by. To turn away from the gospel would be throwing out fullness for emptiness, the substance for the shadow, and the truth for falsehood. May the Holy Spirit continue to lead us even further into the knowledge of Christ crucified. May we never in any way quit our sincere belief in the truth or stop being thankful for it. —*TNSDB*

NOVEMBER 2

THE GOOD SAMARITAN

"Which of these three, do you think, proved to be a neighbor to the man who fell among the robbers?" He said, "The one who showed him mercy." And Jesus said to him, "You go, and do likewise." —Luke 10:36-37

Compassion is a great gospel duty. It must be cheerful and practical. When we see someone in distress, we must not pass by like the priest and Levite did. That would show that our religion is only skin-deep and has never affected our hearts. We must pity, go near, help and become a friend. We must do everything necessary that is within our power and never leave the person in need until we have seen the matter through. The good Samaritan has earned himself everlasting honor. Let us imitate him by showing brotherly love to those who are in trouble, even if they happen to be opposed to our religion or even regard us as enemies. Such behavior will bring glory to God and go a long way toward recommending the holy faith we claim. The Lord help us to do so, for Jesus' sake. Amen. —*TNSDB*

Therefore, since we have been justified by faith, we have peace with God through our Lord Jesus Christ. —Romans 5:1

Faith clings to the righteousness of Jesus that makes us innocent before the Lord. It also brings a heavenly peace into the soul. No confidence in ourselves can ever do this. Our own good works are defective at best. They will never make peace between us and God, nor bring peace to our conscience. What a joy it is to be justified before God and know we are "accepted in the Beloved" (Ephesians 1:6 NKJV). No wonder that the person who is so favored enjoys peace of soul. —*TNSDB*

God's knowing everything is a source of comfort to those losing hope.

Through him we have also obtained access by faith into this grace in which we stand, and we rejoice in hope of the glory of God. —Romans 5:2

Being at perfect peace with God we are allowed to approach him and have complete joy in his presence. Do we know anything about this? Let each of us answer this question personally.

More than that, we rejoice in our sufferings. —Romans 5:3a

Whatever privileges we enjoy, there are more to follow, and we may add, "more than that." We eventually come to the point where we find joy even in our sorrows, because we know they work for our spiritual good. —*TNSDB*

Knowing that suffering produces endurance, and endurance produces character, and character produces hope, and hope does not put us to shame, because God's love has been poured into our hearts through the Holy Spirit who has been given to us. —Romans 5:3b-5

See how one precious stone is arranged next to another, course upon course of priceless jewels; building a heavenly character like the very temple of God. We are that temple, and the love of God comes into us like the divine glory into the holy place, and lights it all up with a heavenly magnificence. Happy is the believer who understands he has all the wealth of heaven! —*TNSDB*

The right thing to do after a good sermon is to put it into practice.

NOVEMBER 6

JESUS

"*Jesus.*" Of all the names of our blessed Lord, this is the most charming to our ear. Well might the Duke of Argyll say, when Samuel Rutherford began to speak on the name Jesus, "Ring that bell again." It has been so dear to Christians that they have tried to make something out of each syllable and even every letter of it. Perhaps some have taken flights of fancy, but, still, it clearly proves that the name was like honey in their mouths and like the sweetest music in their ears.

—Sermon #2592 *The Power of Christ's Name*

THE BOOK SHOULD BE EXAMINED

If there were nothing more than a rumor that a book had been inspired by God, and that it revealed his own character, thoughts and will, then an honest man, wanting to do the right thing, would make sure to quickly discover if the rumor was true. Upon finding such a book he would want to acquire it and carefully examine its claims. The Bible claims to be the Word of God and has been greatly revered for generations. It has been accepted as God's word by so vast a number of wise and righteous men that we cannot talk about its reality as a mere rumor. It has been around for a very long time and has been accepted by many of the best of our race. —*The Clue of the Maze*

Contend, O LORD, with those who contend with me; fight against those who fight against me! —Psalm 35:1

Are you injured at the hands of wicked people? Are you too poor to sue for damages? Does a *Nimrod* oppress you? Does a *Laban* cheat you? Does a greedy landlord complain about you? Well, do not take the matter into your own hands by attempting illegal means. Do not presume to be the judge in your own cause to correct the situation. Always remember what the apostle taught his Thessalonians. "God considers it just to repay with affliction those who afflict you, and to grant relief to you who are afflicted...when the Lord Jesus is revealed from heaven with his mighty angels" (2 Thessalonians 1:6-7). —Isaac Craven's Sermon at Paul's Cross (1630)

Let God be true though every one were a liar. —Romans 3:4

Others may deceive, but God must be true. If all the truth in the whole world could be gathered, it would be only a drop in the bucket compared with the truthfulness of God. The truthfulness of the best of people would amount to nothing compared with the certain truth of God. The faithfulness of the most righteous of people is like a wisp of smoke, but the faithfulness of God is like a rock. If we trust in good people, then we should trust in the good God infinitely more. Why does it seem odd to trust in the promise of God? To many, it looks like a dreamy, sentimental, religious business; but if we consider it calmly, it is the most matter of fact action that can be. —*According to Promise*

---

*Our forgetfulness of mercy in the past is at the heart
of our present hopelessness.*

And when [Jesus] had finished speaking, he said to Simon, "Put out into the deep and let down your nets for a catch." And Simon answered, "Master, we toiled all night and took nothing! But at your word I will let down the nets."

—Luke 5:4-5

Whatever may have happened in the past or how hopeless the future may seem, our job is to obey, and in obeying we will meet with a reward. —*TNSDB*

NOVEMBER 11

Samson was very thirsty after he struck 1,000 Philistines with the jawbone of a donkey **"and he called upon the LORD and said, 'You have granted this great salvation by the hand of your servant, and shall I now die of thirst and fall into the hands of the uncircumcised?' And God split open the hollow place that is at Lehi, and water came out from it."** —Judges 15:18-19

Samson knew how to pray and to pray in faith too. This was the saving point in his character.

God helps his servants in big situations, but sometimes he strengthens their faith by bringing smaller tests into their lives. But he will not leave them alone even in their minor difficulties. He quenched Samson's thirst by bringing a refreshing spring of water right where the jawbone fell from the hero's hand. God never runs low on power. We have only to trust him, and we shall do great things, and receive great things. —*TNSDB*

When we ask why the Lord loved this person of that person, we have to come back to our Savior's answer to that question, "Yes, Father, for such was your gracious will."

NOVEMBER 12

Then Israel said to Joseph, "Behold, I am about to die, but God will be with you and will bring you again to the land of your fathers. —Genesis 48:21

Whoever dies, the Lord remains with his people. Let us not lose hope, even if the best of our friends or the most capable of our pastors are taken from us. —*TNSDB*

All things work together for good. —Romans 8:28

Whether or not faith in God will produce for us what is best worth living for, each person must decide for himself. The likelihood points in that direction. It is reasonable that a man trusting in his maker will find himself mostly benefited by his faith. Some of us are so certain of the excellence of faith that we are content to run the greatest risks that we may face in the future and trust them to God. The many happy experiences that faith has already given us make us confident to face the biggest challenges ahead. We deliberately say, "For God alone, O my soul, wait in silence, for my hope is from him (Psalm 62:5).

—The Clue of the Maze

When Enoch had *lived* 65 years he fathered Methuselah. Enoch walked with God after he fathered Methuselah 300 years and had other sons and daughters. Thus all the days of Enoch were 365 years. Enoch *walked* with God, and he was not, for God took him. —Genesis 5:21-24

It is worth noticing here that the sacred writer says once that Enoch "lived;" but then he changes the word and writes Enoch "walked with God." This teaches us that fellowship with God was the most important thing in Enoch's life. Fellowship with God should also be the most important thing in our lives. Enoch was not a mere talker about God, but a walker with God. This holy patriarch lived in unbroken relationship with the Lord for three hundred years—not visiting with God now and then, but constantly walking with him. This is not an easy thing to do. To remain in unbroken fellowship, "this is the work, this is the labor." Yet the Holy Spirit can enable us to accomplish even this. Continued fellowship is what we should aim at. We should not be satisfied with anything short of it. —*TNSDB*

> **You have given him dominion over the works of your**
> **hands;**
> **you have put all things under his feet,**
> **all sheep and oxen,**
> **and also the beasts of the field,**
> **the birds of the heavens; the fish of the sea,**
> **whatever passes along the paths of the seas.** —Psalm 8:6-7

Mankind either tames these creatures or uses them for food. They all fear man. His power over the animal kingdom is less because of the fall, yet he still walks among the inferior animals with something of that awe, which, as a poet said, "doth hedge a king" [William Shakespeare's *Hamlet*]. In Adam's innocence, man's rule of the animal kingdom was no doubt complete and delightful. One imagines him leaning on a lion, while a fawn frisks at the side of Eve. In the Lord Jesus, however, we see man given the highest place of honor. We know that the situation of our Lord Jesus represents the situation of all his people, because he is the Head and we make up his body. In Jesus man is indeed "crowned with glory and honor" (Hebrews 2:7). It is both our duty and our privilege to rise above all things of earth. We must be careful to keep the world under our feet and animals in their proper place. Let none of us allow having pets to become a snare to us. We are to reign over them. We must not allow them to reign over us.

—TNSDB

When the first Adam had sinned and brought death on the world—had brought a curse on it—he ran away and hid in the bushes. But when the second Adam came to take his place and suffer his guilt, instead of hiding away in the bushes of Gethsemane, he came out and said to these men who were seeking him, "'Whom do you seek?' And they said, 'Jesus of Nazareth.' Jesus answered, 'I told you that I am he.'" He "gave himself for our sins."

The first man was disobedient to the point of death, but the second man was "obedient to the point of death."

—D.L. Moody, *The Two Adams*

I believe; help my unbelief! —Mark 9:24

The truths on which I place my trust are uncomplicated and easily understood, yet the evil of my own heart throws many doubts at them, and I stand amazed that my faith keeps her hold on them. I believe that Christ died for my sins with much more assurance than I believe anything else; no fact in history is one-half so certain to me. And yet, at times, it is so hard to believe it, that it is clear to me that true faith does not come from man, but is a fruit of the Spirit. The truth that forces itself on such morally darkened minds as ours and changes us must be very great!

—Sermon #786 *The Great Mystery of Godliness*

Those who can best afford it should do the most for the honor of our Lord's kingdom.

Great indeed, we confess, is the mystery of godliness.
—1 Timothy 3:16

There is no room for indifference where the gospel is concerned. It is either the most astounding of frauds or the most amazing of revelations. No one can remain undecided about it and be safe. It is too weighty, too serious, to be ignored as a matter of no concern. Enemies and friends alike acknowledge that the mystery of godliness is great. It is not a rippling stream of ideology, but a wide ocean of thought, no molehill of truth, but an Alp of revelation, no single beam of light, but a sun shining at full strength. — Sermon #786 *The Great Mystery of Godliness*

NOVEMBER 19

I give them eternal life, and they will never perish, and no one will snatch them out of my hand. —John 10:28

I cannot advance an inch without praying my way, nor keep the inch I gain without staying on guard and standing fast. Grace alone can preserve and perfect me. The old nature will kill the new nature if it can; and to this moment the only reason why my new nature is not dead is this—because it cannot die. If my new nature could have died, it would have been killed long ago. But Jesus said, "I give [my sheep] eternal life" and "Whoever believes has eternal life." Therefore the believer cannot die.

—Sermon #1850 *Unlimited Love*

NOVEMBER 20

Nevertheless, I tell you the truth: it is to your advantage that I go away, for if I do not go away, the Helper will not come to you. But if I go, I will send him to you. —John 16:7

If Jesus were here in one place, not all of us could reach him. This is one reason the presence of the Holy Spirit is more valuable than if the Redeemer were on earth bodily. The Helper, the Comforter, the Holy Spirit can be in all of the assemblies of the saints at the same time. He can teach all the disciples of the Lord at the same time. He can assist us to pray and inspire tens of thousands of praises at the same time. He can apply the word of God with power to millions of hearts at the same instant. The glory of the church is the unchanging power of the Holy Spirit that comforts the church and influences the world. —*TNSDB*

NOVEMBER 21

Therefore, my beloved, as you have always obeyed, so now, not only as in my presence but much more in my absence, work out your own salvation with fear and trembling, for it is God who works in you, both to will and to work for his good pleasure.—Philippians 2:12-13

We work out what the Lord works in. The grace of God is not an excuse to be idle. It is a reason to be hard working! God gives us both the will to work and the work to do. Therefore, let us will with strong determination and work with fearless persistence. This is how we will fulfill the good pleasure of the Lord. —*TNSDB*

The saints of God are always watched by the world, and this should make them all the more careful in their behavior.

NOVEMBER 22

For the wages of sin is death, but the free gift of God is eternal life in Christ Jesus our Lord. —Romans 6:23

We no longer work for wages. Everything we receive is a gift. Therefore let gratitude cause us to obey, and compel us to be holy before the Lord. The person who lives under the law works to be good for what he can get out of it. Gratitude for God's eternal love will be a far greater force in our hearts. By the help of the Holy Spirit, we will abound in good works because grace abounds in our lives. —*TNSDB*

[The kingdom of heaven will be] like a man going on a journey, who called his servants and entrusted to them his property. To one he gave five talents, to another two, to another one, to each according to his ability. Then he went away….He who had received the one talent went and dug in the ground and hid his master's money. —Matthew 25:14-15, 18

We all have some talent. It may be only one, but we are responsible for it. Are we using it to the measure of our ability? Many wish they had more talents, but this is wrong. The Lord has entrusted us with just the number of gifts we can handle properly. Our great concern should be to be found faithful managers of that which has been placed in our care.

The "wicked and slothful servant" probably thought that because he could not do much he would not do anything. There are thousands who think the same way. They believe that their little is not needed and will never be missed, and therefore they make no attempt to serve their Lord. Are we like that? He was not rebellious, just lazy, but that condemned him. —*TNSDB*

We know that our old self was crucified with him.
—Romans 6:6

The believer was buried with Christ and those who are dead are free from the law that condemned them. How can the law arrest a dead person? So, we who are dead in Christ and risen again in him are new creatures, and do not come under the divine sentence. God now knows us not as sinners, but as new creatures in Christ Jesus. He knows and recognizes in us the new life, because "he has caused us to be born again to a living hope through the resurrection of Jesus Christ from the dead." That is one of the instructive features of baptism. In baptism the believer pictures the doctrine of salvation by death and burial. —Sermon #1142 *Free Pardon*

WE ARE SURE TO SUCCEED when we can appeal to a promise. It is good to say to the Lord, "Do as you have said." There is great force in a prayer that appeals to the word, the promise, and the covenant of God. If someone presents a promissory note on the day that it is due, he expects to receive the amount indicated. God's promises are promissory notes and he will honor them. He has never dishonored a promise yet and he never will. If you can just quote a promise that applies to your situation, and spread it before the Lord in faith, and say, "Remember this promise to your servant on which you have caused me to hope," you must obtain the blessing. Pleading the promise gives such a knock at the gate of heaven that it must be opened. —Sermon #1723 *Knock*

Pastors are not sent to please us, but to guide us.

May the Lord of peace himself give you peace at all times in every way. —2 Thessalonians 3:16

The apostle Paul saw that the Thessalonians were greatly troubled and he wrote the most encouraging words to cheer them. But he knew that he could not lift the burden from their hearts. So he turned to the God of all comfort and asked him to give them "peace at all times in every way." The weakness of our power to bless others will bring no harm to them if it leads us to take hold of eternal strength, because that will bring a superior power on the field to bless. Our inability will only make room for divine grace to be seen. —Sermon # 2679 *Christ's Indwelling Word*

KILLING TIME

There are people who talk about killing and say they like to read novels to kill time. But a good Christian does not need to do that; they never have enough time. Why, if there were forty-eight hours instead of twenty-four in a day and night, we would still want more time to work for the Lord. It is only a little while, a few days and hours, that we stay here and we have to do all that is given us to do in that short time. No child of God should talk about killing time.

I have one rule about books. I do not read any book, unless it will help me to understand *the* book. I want to tell you right here, that there is not anything that I have to give up. It is a great pleasure to get a book that helps unfold the blessed Bible. It is manna to my soul. If you young converts get in love with the Bible it will help you wonderfully. I advise you to join a good Bible class, and to get experienced Christians to help you. Go there and learn, and then go out and help teach others, and you will grow in grace as a result. —D. L. Moody, *Message to Young Converts*

NOVEMBER 28

…Epaphras our beloved fellow servant. He is a faithful minister of Christ on your behalf and has made known to us your love in the Spirit. —Colossians 1:7-8

It is delightful to hear one servant of God praise another like this. There is far too little of this in our day. True soldiers of Christ have a high regard for their comrades and are glad to promote their good reputation. Paul praises Epaphras to the Colossians as his way of recommending that worthy brother to them. Anything less may have destroyed his influence on them and injured the cause of Christ as a result. —*TNSDB*

NOVEMBER 29

Peace to all of you who are in Christ. —1 Peter 5:14

This blessing is given to all in Christ Jesus, but to no one else. "'There is no peace,' says my God, 'for the wicked'" (Isaiah 57:21). Those who are outside of Christ share restlessness here and misery forever. Oh Lord, let no one in this family remain without faith in Jesus. —*TNSDB*

NOVEMBER 30

You desire and do not have, so you murder. You covet and cannot obtain, so you fight and quarrel. You do not have, because you do not ask. —James 4:2

Praying is better than fighting. If God will give us what we ask for, why do we feel the need to fight for it?

You ask and do not receive, because you ask wrongly, to spend it on your own passions. —James 4:3

If anyone says that they have prayed and not received, their motive was clearly selfish, and therefore God would not indulge them. —*TNSDB*

DECEMBER 1

Whatever is true, whatever is honorable, whatever is just, whatever is pure, whatever is lovely, whatever is commendable, if there is any excellence, if there is anything worthy of praise, think about these things. —Philippians 4:8

Paul gives us a lot to think about. Take each word and study it, and then put it in practice. Every member of the family should learn this verse by heart. It is a big book on virtue pressed into a very tiny space. —*TNSDB*

The mission that is carried on in the spirit of prayer will certainly end well.

DECEMBER 2

Peace I leave with you. —John 14:27

The truly restful state of mind is enjoyed when the heart and life are cleansed by grace. This must be done daily so there is nothing to grieve the Spirit of God, and therefore the Lord feels right in favoring his child with the light of his cheerful face in its full noonday splendor. Oh how wonderful to relax in the sunlight of Jehovah's love, free from all doubt, and not bothered about sin! The contentment of heaven lies in that conscious sense of having God's favor. May the Lord of peace himself give us this peace.

—Sermon #1343 *The Jewel of Peace*

December 3

A good name is better than precious ointment, and the day of death than the day of birth. —Ecclesiastes 7:1

Almost everyone would like to have a good reputation. To be known as a righteous person is a good reason for choosing to live a life of integrity. And to have died as a martyr for the faith, or to have lived as a persecuted believer, or endured poverty rather than undermine Christian principles is a great blessing. To die being remembered for holiness and kindness means the difficult trials of life were worth it. To these, the day of death is the completing of a life of honor, the celebration of a life lived well. —*TNSDB*

December 4

And they were bringing children to [Jesus] that he might touch them, and the disciples rebuked them. But when Jesus saw it, he was indignant and said to them, "Let the children come to me; do not hinder them, for to such belongs the kingdom of God. Truly, I say to you, whoever does not receive the kingdom of God like a child shall not enter it." And he took them in his arms and blessed them, laying his hands on them. —Mark 10:13-16

No doubt, the mothers of these children believed that the Savior's blessing would enrich their children in the best way. They felt it would lead to their future happiness and so they brought their boys and girls to him. The disciples thought that he would be annoyed with the little ones. They had not yet learned what a kind heart he had. No fathers or mothers should think their children are too young to be converted. Jesus can bless them while they are still boys and girls.

We do not often find Jesus displeased about something. Therefore, we should learn from this that, beyond all other things, discouraging a child from coming to Jesus is displeasing to him. We must possess the simplicity, teachability, and trust of children, or else grace is not in us. Like them, we must also be free from greediness and ambition. —*TNSDB*

DECEMBER 5

The kingdom of heaven is like treasure hidden in a field, which a man found and covered up. Then in his joy he goes and sells all that he has and buys that field.

Again, the kingdom of heaven is like a merchant in search of fine pearls, who, on finding one pearl of great value, went and sold all that he had and bought it. —Matthew 13:44-46

The first man represents the sinner who is converted suddenly. He finds Jesus even though he was not looking for him. The second man is the diligent seeker who has been seeking Jesus and finally discovers him. They both agree that their treasure is of the highest value. Do we value Jesus like this? Is he very precious to our hearts? —*TNSDB*

Someone who is not loyal to his friends is probably someone who is not loyal to the Savior.

DECEMBER 6

But when [Uzziah] was strong, he grew proud, to his destruction. —2 Chronicles 26:16

What a warning this is to Christians who are well off. When we are weak we depend on the Lord and are safe. But when we are strong the temptation is to become proud and then a fall is near. More fall among the strong than among the timid and trembling.

—TNSDB

DECEMBER 7

When he has tried me, I shall come out as gold. —Job 23:10

I do not know what troubles may come, nor what temptations may surface; but I know in whose hands I am, and I am persuaded that he is able to care for me. "When he has tried me." I will go into the fire, but I will not be burned up in it. "I shall come out." Like the three holy children, though the furnace is heated seven times hotter, yet the Son of man will be with me in the furnace, and "I shall come out" with not even the smell of fire on me. Yes, "I shall come out," and no one can stop me. It is good to begin with this holy confidence and let that confidence increase as you get closer to the final reward. Has God not promised that we will never perish? Will we not, therefore, come out as gold?

—Sermon #2098 *Where Are You Going?*

DECEMBER 8

He will bless those who fear the LORD, both the small and the great. —Psalm 115:13

The small are mentioned first in the verse and so ranked first. Perhaps this to show that though they may be slighted and paid little attention to by the world, yet they are great in the eyes of the Lord.

Will only great saints receive the kingdom and everlasting glory? Will only great works be rewarded, only those works that are accomplished by great grace and the abundance of the gifts of the Holy Spirit? No! "Whoever gives one of these little ones even a cup of cold water because he is a disciple, truly, I say to you, he will by no means lose his (a disciple's) reward" (Matthew 10:42).

—John Bunyan, *The Fear of God*

DECEMBER 9

FAITH MUST NOT BE COMBINED WITH OTHER THINGS

There is a tendency among those who aim for a holy life to mix their faith in God with other things. They are eager to enjoy every aid to faith and this tends to make them want to support the Rock of Ages with timber from their own forests. However this will only lead to confusion. If we trust God at all we must trust him completely. The highest power includes every other power, and therefore the idea of supplementing the power of the living God is as foolish as it is insulting. Do I trust in God to save me from sin in his own promised way? Then I must believe that he will fulfill his promise no matter how I feel inside. God is to be believed. He cannot change or fall short. —*The Clue of the Maze*

DECEMBER 10

They have no root in themselves, but endure for a while.
—Mark 4:17

With a genuine Christian there is always as much underground as there is above ground. This underground work is often very neglected, but it is extremely important; indeed, it is essential. One of the roots of a true Christian is secret repentance; secret prayer is another. These are roots that run deep into the soil. The person who does not have these has no root. Secret unity with God, the heart talking with the great Father, the secret pouring of self out in heartfelt fellowship and praise, is part of this hidden root system. The inner life, which none of our neighbors can see, everything that is the most important part of us, is essential.

· —Sermon #2846 *No Root in Themselves*

December 11

My soul is in the midst of lions; I lie down amid fiery beasts—the children of man, whose teeth are spears and arrows, whose tongues are sharp swords. My heart is steadfast, O God, my heart is steadfast! I will sing and make melody! —Psalm 57:4, 7

Under the circumstances, one would have thought David would say, "My heart is trembling." But no! He is calm, firm, happy, determined, and aware that he is accepted by God. When the central axle is secure, the wheels works well. When the ship's main anchor holds, the ship cannot drift away. "My heart is steadfast, O God." I am committed to trust you, to serve you, and to praise you. He repeats himself to give glory to the God who comforts the souls of those who serve him. Surely it will be well with each one of us if we take our drifting hearts and anchor them securely on God and proclaim his glory. "I will sing and make melody!" With my voice and with instruments, I will worship and celebrate you, my Lord and God! With my lips and my heart I will give you the credit. Satan shall not stop me. I will make the town ring with music and echo in joyful praise. —*TNSDB*

December 12

Let a righteous man strike me—it is a kindness;
let him rebuke me—it is oil for my head;
let my head not refuse it. —Psalm 141:5

It requires great grace to rebuke someone correctly. It takes even more grace to receive a rebuke with the proper attitude. Wise men are thankful when their errors are pointed out to them. Unfortunately, there are very few wise men. —*TNSDB*

He gives more grace. —James 4:6

You grow, but that growth is God's gift and you must look to him for it.

Why did the Lord not give us the largest measure of grace to begin with? Why promise more grace later? I think it is because we value grace all the more when it comes to us little by little. It is for our own good to be required to put forth effort to get more grace. A poor woman is allowed to go and glean in a field. Your generosity might say, "Come, my good woman, I will give you the wheat and you will not have to bother gleaning." But this might not be such a good a thing for her as to allow her to gather the wheat by her own efforts. It is often much better to enable the poor to help themselves than to help them without their own efforts. God is wise toward us. He intends to give us the wheat, but he decides that we must make the effort to glean it; and in doing so he increases our godliness. We are to become rich in grace, but it is to be done heaven's way. Growth in grace is a gift; remember that. God's grace is received, not as some dead external thing, but as a living outgrowth of the inner spiritual life.

—Sermon #1488 *More & More, or Less & Less*

You shall love the Lord your God with all your heart and with all your soul and with all your strength and with all your mind. —Luke 120:27

These words sound to me like great strokes of the soul's engine! They urge us to move forward in the holy voyage. Brothers and sisters, our life is a race, we must run in it. It must be hard running, too. "Let us also lay aside every weight, and sin which clings so closely, and let us run with endurance the race that is set before us." If we are really on the right course, let us move forward with all our powers; and may God help us so we can win the prize!

—Sermon #2098 *Where Are You Going?*

DECEMBER 15

Help me with your salvation. —Psalm 106:4 (Alternate reading)

Now, poor trembling one, let me whisper a word in your ear. May the Holy Spirit give you comfort with it. If you have a broken heart, you do not need to say, "Lord, help me." Do you not know that he lives in you? Is it not written, "This is the one to whom I will look; he who is humble and contrite in spirit and trembles at my word"? Are you not that very person? I wish you could rejoice at God's word, but since you cannot, I am glad you tremble at it. You are the one with whom God has promised to live. "Trembles at my word." Take hold of that. Believe that the Lord looks in your direction and is with you.

—Sermon #1454 *A Poor Man's Prayer*

DECEMBER 16

Although he was a son, he learned obedience through what he suffered. And being made perfect, he became the source of eternal salvation to all who obey him. —Hebrews 5:8-9

A perfected Savior provides all believers with a perfect and everlasting salvation. He was always perfect in character, but his life of sorrow on earth completely qualifies him for the office of Savior, in a way nothing else could. Who would not obey a Master who has undergone all kinds of sorrow so he would be able to sympathize with his servants? Who would not want a salvation that was won by one who was "made lower than the angels" (Hebrews 2:9) for our sake? *—TNSDB*

DECEMBER 17

I charge you in the presence of God and of Christ Jesus…preach the word; be ready in season and out of season; reprove, rebuke, and exhort, with complete patience and teaching. —2 Timothy 4:1-2

A minister is never off duty. He should not only win souls whenever an opportunity presents itself, but he should also make opportunities. Reliable teaching and zeal must go together in equal proportions. Dr. Ryland well said, "No sermon is likely to be useful that does not have the three **R**'s in it: **R**uin by the Fall; **R**edemption by Christ; **R**egeneration by the Holy Spirit. My goal in every sermon is to call sinners, to stir up the saints, and to be made a blessing to all." —*TNSDB*

True faith produces a spirit that is not dependent on others.

DECEMBER 18

Now there are many people that have love and they hold the truth. I should have said they have truth, but they don't hold it in love, and they are very unsuccessful in working for God. They are very harsh, and God cannot use them. Now let us hold the truth, but let us hold it in love. People will stand almost any kind of sincere talk if you only do it in love. If you do it in harshness it bounces back and they won't receive it. So what we want is to have the truth and at the same time to hold it in love.

—D. L. Moody, *Christian Love*

December 19

Wisdom is good with an inheritance, an advantage to those who see the sun. For the protection of wisdom is like the protection of money, and the advantage of knowledge is that wisdom preserves the life of him who has it.

—Ecclesiastes 7:11-12

Oh, the depth of the riches and wisdom and knowledge of God! —Romans 11:33

People who have an inheritance and no wisdom are in a sad situation. With wealth comes great responsibilities, but they have no grace to measure up to them. The truest wealth is true religion. The richest person is the one who has God for their inheritance.

If we understand that the wisdom Solomon is talking about is true wisdom, which is real godliness, then his meaning becomes clear. There is no real life apart from faith in the Lord Jesus. Faith is our best protection in this life, as well as the greatest way to live.

—TNSDB

December 20

Wrath is cruel, anger is overwhelming, but who can stand before jealousy? —Proverbs 27:4

Adam and Satan both fell because they envied God. If we give in to jealousy, it will certainly take away our happiness. Envy spits its venom on the best of people. It is a horrible and devilish emotion. Those who follow the loving Jesus must fight against resentment and overcome it. *—TNSDB*

DECEMBER 21

For my iniquities have gone over my head; like a heavy burden, they are too heavy for me. —Psalm 38:4

It is undeniable, that the backslidings of the holy men of God, as recorded in the Holy Bible, are of great use to us. Spots are nowhere more offensive than when seen on a beautiful face, or on the cleanest garment. And it is profitable for us to have a perfect understanding of the filthiness of sin. We also learn from them to keep a low opinion of ourselves, to depend on the grace of God, and to keep a stricter eye on ourselves, lest perhaps we fall into the same or worse sins (Galatians 6:1). —Herman Witsius (1636-1708)

DECEMBER 22

The time of the promise drew near. —Acts 7:17a

The time for its fulfillment is an important part of a promise. Indeed, it is part of its essence. It would be wrong to delay making a scheduled payment; and the obligation to keep one's word is much the same. The Lord is prompt to the moment in keeping his gracious appointments. The Lord threatened to destroy the world with a flood, but he delayed bringing the waters over the earth until Noah had entered the ark; and then "on that day all the fountains of the great deep burst forth, and the windows of the heavens were opened." The Lord declared that Israel would come out of Egypt, and it happened. "At the end of 430 years, on that very day, all the hosts of the LORD went out from the land of Egypt" (Exodus 12:41).

As for the greatest promise of all, that is, the sending of his Son from heaven, the Lord was not late with that great gift, "But when the fullness of time had come, God sent forth his Son, born of woman." The Lord our God keeps his word down to the very moment. It is beyond all question. —*According to Promise*

DECEMBER 23

Now may the Lord of peace himself give you peace.

—2 Thessalonians 3:16

"Now may the Lord of peace himself give you peace." Who is this "Lord of peace"? The Lord Jesus, the Prince of peace, born into the world when the entire world was at peace. It was only a short pause when the gates of the temple of war were closed, and lo, Jesus came to Bethlehem, and angels sang, "And on earth peace." He came to establish an empire of peace that will be universal. Under his reign the useless battle helmet will be put away and war will be studied no more. "Prince of Peace!" How blessed is that title! So wrote Isaiah of old, and Paul, the true successor of Isaiah, changing just one word, now speaks of "the Lord of peace." —Sermon #1343 *The Jewel of Peace*

DECEMBER 24

I will thank you in the great congregation; in the mighty throng I will praise you. —Psalm 35:18

Noteworthy deliverances must be remembered, their importance impressed on our minds. All of the saints should be informed about the Lord's goodness. The theme is worthy of the largest audience; the experience of a believer is a subject suitable for an assembled universe to hear about. Most people talk about their miseries, good people should proclaim their mercies. I will glorify the God of my salvation among friends and foes. Praise—personal praise, public praise, perpetual praise—should be the daily rent paid to the King of heaven. *—The Treasury of David*

> **Bless the LORD, all his works,**
> **in all places of his dominion.**
> **Bless the LORD, O my soul!** —Psalm 103:22

The psalmist was so full of praise that he wanted all of creation to join him in glorifying the Lord. But he did not forget that the most important thing is that our own soul adores the Lord. He concludes, as all good composers do, with his main point. Let our motto be today and every day, "Bless the Lord, O my soul."

—TNSDB

> **How long, O Lord, will you look on? Rescue me from their**
> **destruction, My precious life from the lions!** —Psalm 35:17

"Why are you a mere spectator? Why are neglecting your servant? Are you not concerned? 'Do you not care that we are perishing?'" (Mark 4:38). We may reason like this with the Lord; he permits this kind of familiarity. There is a time for our salvation, but our impatience often thinks it is very slow in coming. Yet wisdom has determined the hour, and nothing will delay it. "Lord, be pleased to set me free from their many assaults and the evil plans they have against me. Rescue my precious soul from my attackers." His enemies were fierce, cunning, and as strong as young lions; only God could deliver him from their jaws. Therefore he addresses himself to God. *—The Treasury of David*

DECEMBER 27

WHEN MARY AND JOSEPH BROUGHT JESUS TO THE TEMPLE

And when the time came for their purification according to the Law of Moses, they brought him up to Jerusalem to present him to the Lord...and to offer a sacrifice according to what is said in the Law of the Lord, "a pair of turtledoves, or two young pigeons." —Luke 2:22, 24

For our sakes, our Lord placed himself under the law and obeyed it in every detail. The poverty of his parents is shown by their presenting the second poorest offering accepted by the law. We know they were not in the worst poverty, because there was one offering even lower than theirs.[1] That greatest hardship was reserved for Jesus when he left home, began his ministry and had "nowhere to lay his head" (Luke 9:58). "Though he was rich, yet for your sake he became poor" (2 Corinthians 8:9). —*TNSDB*

[1] "A person could bring two turtledoves or two young pigeons as a burnt offering; (Leviticus 5:7), or, in extreme cases he might even substitute a tenth of an ephah of fine flour (verses 11-13)."

—*The Zondervan Pictorial Encyclopedia of the Bible*, Volume 5, page 203.

DECEMBER 28

The wage of the righteous lead to life, the gain of the wicked to sin. —Proverbs 10:16

Work, not idleness, is the badge of a servant of God. With the wicked, it is always "what's in it for me?" Their actions are sinful in the sight of the Lord.

Oh Lord, cause us to work because of the life of Christ within us and give us life even more abundantly. —*TNSDB*

"What peaceful hours I then enjoyed,
How sweet their memory still!
But they have left an aching void,
The world can never fill."

What a great mercy that the world cannot fill that void in our soul, and what a greater mercy that God will fill it, because he never emptied a soul he did not intend to fill, he never stripped a man he did not mean to clothe, he never made someone a spiritual beggar without intending to make that person spiritually rich; and if you are brought to the first stage of desperation today, then you are brought to the first stage of hope. When a person comes to their wit's end, God will begin to display his mercy and his truth!

—Sermon #440 *Cheer for the Fainthearted*

The path of faith is not an easy one,
but it is always the safest one.

DECEMBER 30

This is my comfort in my affliction, that your promise gives me life. —Psalm 119:50

Good people will have times of suffering. Their best comfort at these times is the shining grace of God. Instead of praying, "Lord, remove the trouble," we should cry, "Lord, give the grace promised in your word." —*TNSDB*

Why should the nations say, "Where is their God?" Our God is in the heavens; he does all that he pleases.

—Psalm 115:2-3

The enemies of God complain about him and blame him for their troubles. The saints of God mention these blasphemies in their prayers and ask the Lord to shut the mouths of these bitter persons. No matter how much the ungodly may rage, God sits upon the throne. They cannot overthrow him from his position of control over them. The most violent efforts to defeat God will not stop him from accomplishing everything he intends to do. Every plan of the Lord will be completed, right down to the smallest detail. This is sweet comfort for his saints. —*TNSDB*

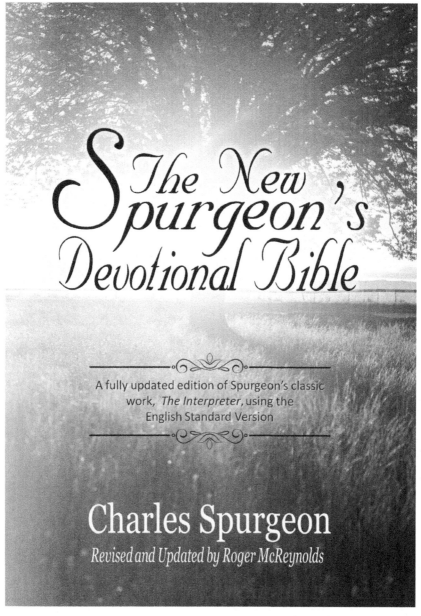

The New Spurgeon's Devotional Bible

A fully updated edition of Spurgeon's classic work, *The Interpreter*, using the English Standard Version

Charles Spurgeon
Revised and Updated by Roger McReynolds

The New Spurgeon's Devotional Bible is a 600,000 word, two year, daily devotional for use in family worship time. This unabridged edition has been fully Updated for Today's Readers; Scripture is in the English Standard Version.

Available in paperback and eBook editions at Amazon.com.

Made in the USA
Monee, IL
06 December 2020